# BADEN WÜRTT

## TRAVEL GUIDE

Your Travel Companion To Wander, Explore, And Savor The Highlights Of This Must-Visit Destination

Lawrence P. Hardy

Copyright © 2025 Lawrence P. Hardy
All Rights Reserved.

# PLEASE READ ME!

**Thank you for choosing our travel guide.** We are committed to providing comprehensive and reliable travel insights, ensuring that the information presented is as accurate as possible. However, travel conditions can change quickly and unexpectedly.

We recognize that travelers depend on our guide for trip planning and decision-making. While we strive for precision, details such as operating hours, pricing, and service availability may differ from what is listed. We strongly recommend verifying essential information, particularly for time-sensitive activities, reservations, or scheduled plans.

**Your safety is our priority. We encourage you to stay aware of your surroundings, exercise standard travel precautions, and remain informed about local conditions.** Each destination has its own unique characteristics and challenges, so it's important to follow current guidelines, respect local customs, and make choices based on your comfort level.

**You may notice that some information appears in multiple sections of this guide. This is intentional, as most travelers refer to different topics as needed rather than reading straight through.** For example, restaurant details may be found in both the dining section and must-visit listings, while safety guidelines may be included in general advice and specific neighborhood descriptions. **This strategic repetition minimizes the need for constant cross-referencing, ensuring you have the key details whenever and wherever you need them.**

Feel free to explore the guide in any order—each section is designed as a complete resource, allowing you to plan your journey smoothly without flipping between pages.

# TRAVEL MAP

## SCAN QR CODE FOR MAP & MEDIA

- Open your QR code scanner (download one from your app store if needed).
- Aim your camera at the QR code to scan it.
- Tap the link that appears after scanning to access the map.
- The link will direct you to the map of your travel destination.
- When prompted, allow the map to access your location for accurate navigation.

- On the map, click "Directions" to get detailed instructions to your destination.
- For the starting point, select "Your Location" (this may require granting location access to your device).
- For the destination, type in the specific location from this guide that you are heading to.

## TO ACCESS MEDIA

Scroll down to see the "Photos" or "Videos" section after the map page has come up. With this, you will be able to see other tourists reviews and ratings who have previously visited the destinations and establishments.

# TABLE OF CONTENTS

PLEASE READ ME!

TRAVEL MAP

SCAN QR CODE FOR MAP & MEDIA

| | |
|---|---|
| TABLE OF CONTENTS | 1 |
| **CHAPTER 1. INTRODUCTION** | **6** |
| Overview of Baden-Württemberg | 6 |
| Why Visit? Highlights of the Region | 9 |
| Brief History and Cultural Significance | 12 |
| Best Time to Visit | 15 |
| **CHAPTER 2. GETTING THERE** | **20** |
| International and Domestic Airports | 20 |
| Train and Bus Connections | 24 |
| Driving Routes and Car Rentals | 28 |
| Visa and Entry Requirements | 31 |
| **CHAPTER 3. LOCAL TRANSPORTATION** | **34** |
| Public Transport: Trams, Buses & Trains | 34 |
| Car Rentals and Driving Tips | 36 |
| Biking and Walking Routes | 41 |
| Taxi and Ride-Sharing Services | 45 |
| **CHAPTER 4. ACCOMMODATION OPTIONS** | **50** |
| Luxury Hotels and Resorts | 50 |
| Mid-Range Hotels & Boutique Stays | 53 |

| | |
|---|---|
| BUDGET STAYS: HOSTELS & GUESTHOUSES | 56 |
| UNIQUE STAYS: CASTLES, FARM STAYS & SPA RESORTS | 59 |

## CHAPTER 5. RESTAURANTS, FOOD & DINING, MUST-TASTE CUISINES — 64

| | |
|---|---|
| MUST-TASTE CUISINES: | 64 |
| BEST RESTAURANTS IN BADEN-WÜRTTEMBERG | 67 |

## CHAPTER 6. MUST-SEE ATTRACTIONS & HIDDEN GEMS — 72

| | |
|---|---|
| HIDDEN GEMS: | 75 |
| TRADITIONAL SWABIAN FESTIVALS & EVENTS | 80 |
| WINE TASTING IN THE VINEYARDS OF BADEN | 84 |
| THERMAL SPAS & WELLNESS RETREATS | 87 |
| FOLK MUSIC AND DANCE PERFORMANCES | 91 |
| EXPLORING HISTORIC TOWNS AND VILLAGES | 95 |
| COOKING CLASSES FOR LOCAL SPECIALTIES | 99 |

## CHAPTER 8. NIGHTLIFE & ENTERTAINMENT — 104

| | |
|---|---|
| BEST BARS & COCKTAIL LOUNGES | 104 |
| LIVE MUSIC VENUES AND CONCERT HALLS | 108 |
| THEATERS, OPERA HOUSES & PERFORMING ARTS | 111 |
| CASINOS AND LATE-NIGHT ENTERTAINMENT | 115 |

## CHAPTER 9. SHOPPING & SOUVENIRS — 120

| | |
|---|---|
| HIGH-END SHOPPING STREETS & MALLS | 120 |
| LOCAL MARKETS AND ARTISAN CRAFTS | 123 |
| BEST PLACES FOR BLACK FOREST CUCKOO CLOCKS | 128 |
| TRADITIONAL SOUVENIRS & WHERE TO BUY THEM | 131 |

## CHAPTER 10. PRACTICAL INFORMATION — 136

| | |
|---|---|
| CURRENCY, ATMS & PAYMENT OPTIONS | 136 |

| Safety Tips & Emergency Contacts | 139 |
| Local Etiquette and Customs | 141 |
| Public Holidays and Festivals | 144 |

## CHAPTER 11. SUGGESTED ITINERARIES — 150

| 3-Day Itinerary: City Highlights of Stuttgart & Heidelberg | 150 |
| 5-Day Itinerary: Black Forest & Lake Constance Adventure | 154 |
| 7-Day Itinerary: Best of Baden-Württemberg (Castles, Nature & Culture) | 159 |

## CONCLUSION — 164

| Final Travel Tips & Recommendations | 164 |

## TRAVEL REFLECTIONS — 168

# CHAPTER 1.

# INTRODUCTION

## Overview of Baden-Württemberg

Baden-Württemberg is a powerhouse of natural beauty, medieval history, automotive innovation, and gastronomic excellence. Nestled between France, Switzerland, and Bavaria, this federal state offers everything from picturesque vineyards and the mystical Black Forest to vibrant cities like Stuttgart, Heidelberg, and Freiburg. Whether you're an outdoor enthusiast, a history buff, or a lover of fine dining, Baden-Württemberg delivers an unparalleled travel experience.

**Geographical and Cultural Diversity**

Baden-Württemberg's landscapes range from the rolling hills of the Swabian Jura to the glistening waters of Lake Constance and the dense, legendary Black Forest. It is a region where medieval castles stand alongside cutting-edge automotive factories, where thermal spas have soothed visitors since Roman times, and where half-timbered towns host centuries-old festivals.

The cultural diversity of Baden-Württemberg is a result of its historic past. The region blends Swabian, Alemannic, and Franconian influences, which are evident in the architecture, dialects, traditions, and, most importantly, the cuisine. Each subregion has its own identity, ensuring that travelers never run out of new experiences.

**Stuttgart: The Dynamic Capital**
- **Address:** Stuttgart, Baden-Württemberg, Germany
- **Opening Hours:** City attractions generally open from 10:00 AM – 6:00 PM
- **Pricing:** Varies; major museums charge €5–€12, while some attractions are free

Stuttgart, the capital of Baden-Württemberg, is a hub of industry and culture. Known as the birthplace of the automobile, it is home to the **Mercedes-Benz Museum** (€12, 9:00 AM – 6:00 PM, closed Mondays) and **Porsche Museum** (€10, 9:00 AM – 6:00 PM, closed Mondays). Beyond cars, Stuttgart boasts **Wilhelma Zoo and Botanical Garden** (€20, open daily 8:15 AM – 6:00 PM) and the regal **Neues Schloss (New Palace)**, a baroque marvel dominating the city center.

For panoramic city views, **Killesberg Park** and the **Stuttgart TV Tower (€10, 10:00 AM – 10:00 PM)** provide breathtaking perspectives. Stuttgart is also a cultural hotspot, hosting the renowned **Staatsgalerie Stuttgart** (€7, 10:00 AM – 5:00 PM, closed Mondays), featuring masterpieces from Rembrandt to Picasso.

**The Black Forest: Myth and Natural Splendor**
- **Key Locations:** Triberg, Baden-Baden, Freiburg
- **Best Visiting Time:** May – October (hiking), December (Christmas markets)

The **Black Forest (Schwarzwald)** is a place of legend, home to dense evergreen forests, cuckoo clocks, and spa towns. **Triberg**, famous for Germany's highest waterfalls (open year-round, €8 entry), also hosts traditional workshops crafting world-famous cuckoo clocks.

For relaxation, **Baden-Baden** offers world-class thermal spas, including **Caracalla Spa (€23 for 2 hours, 8:00 AM – 10:00 PM)** and the historic **Friedrichsbad (€35, 9:00 AM – 10:00 PM)**, where Roman-Irish bathing traditions continue.

For a cultural experience, **Freiburg im Breisgau**, known as the "Jewel of the Black Forest," features **Freiburg Minster Cathedral** (free entry, 10:00 AM – 5:00 PM) and **Schauinsland Cable Car (€15 round trip, 9:00 AM – 5:00 PM)** for stunning mountain views.

### Heidelberg: The Romantic City

- **Key Attraction:** Heidelberg Castle
- **Address:** Schloss Heidelberg, 69117 Heidelberg
- **Opening Hours:** 10:00 AM – 5:30 PM
- **Entry Fee:** €9 adults, €4.50 children

Heidelberg is one of Germany's most picturesque cities, attracting poets, scholars, and artists for centuries. Its centerpiece is **Heidelberg Castle**, a majestic ruin overlooking the Neckar River. The **Philosopher's Walk**, offering sweeping views of the Old Town, is a must-do. The city's **Old Bridge (Alte Brücke)** and **Heidelberg University**, Germany's oldest, add to its historic charm.

### Lake Constance: A Lakeside Paradise

- **Main Cities:** Konstanz, Meersburg, Friedrichshafen
- **Best Activities:** Boat cruises, cycling, visiting Mainau Island

The shimmering **Lake Constance (Bodensee)**, shared with Switzerland and Austria, is a haven for nature lovers. **Mainau Island (€22, 9:00 AM – 7:00 PM)** is renowned for its floral gardens and butterfly house. **Friedrichshafen's Zeppelin Museum (€11, 10:00 AM – 5:00 PM)** showcases the region's aviation history. Cycling along the **Bodensee-Radweg**, a scenic lakeside path, is a must for outdoor enthusiasts.

### Culinary Excellence and Dining

- **Best Restaurant for Fine Dining: Schwarzwaldstube (Baiersbronn)** – 3 Michelin Stars (€250+ per person)

- **Best for Traditional Cuisine: Gasthof Krone (Weinstadt)** – Authentic Swabian dishes (€15–€30 per meal)
- **Best Café Experience: Café König (Baden-Baden)** – Famous for Black Forest Cake (€6 per slice)

Baden-Württemberg is Germany's top culinary destination, boasting **nine three-Michelin-starred restaurants**. The Swabian specialties— **Maultaschen** (stuffed pasta), **Spätzle** (egg noodles), and **Zwiebelrostbraten** (onion roast)—are essential tastings.

**Accommodation Options**
- **Luxury Stay: Brenners Park-Hotel & Spa (Baden-Baden)** – 5-star wellness retreat (€450+ per night)
- **Mid-Range: Hotel Heiligenstein (Baden-Baden)** – Elegant and comfortable (€130 per night)
- **Budget: Jugendherberge Stuttgart** – Well-located youth hostel (€40 per night)

Baden-Württemberg provides a wide range of accommodation, from **castle hotels** to cozy guesthouses. Spa towns like **Baden-Baden** cater to luxury travelers, while charming vineyard stays in the **Swabian Wine Route** offer an authentic local experience.

## Why Visit? Highlights of the Region

A Region of Stunning Contrasts

What makes Baden-Württemberg truly special is its diversity. Whether you seek the romantic charm of Heidelberg, the dense woodlands of the Black Forest, or the contemporary energy of Stuttgart, there's something for every traveler. Unlike many other regions in Germany, Baden-Württemberg offers a rare combination of urban excitement and rural tranquility, making it an ideal destination for both adventure seekers and those looking to unwind.

The Black Forest: An Icon of Natural Beauty

- **Key Locations:** Triberg, Baden-Baden, Feldberg, Baiersbronn
- **Opening Hours:** Open year-round
- **Pricing:** Free access to hiking trails; spa entry fees vary (€15–€40)

The Black Forest (Schwarzwald) is perhaps the most famous natural landmark in the region. Known for its dense pine forests, fairy-tale villages, and thermal spas, this region is a haven for hikers, nature lovers, and those seeking wellness experiences. Visit **Triberg**, home to Germany's highest waterfalls, or **Baiersbronn**, a culinary hotspot featuring multiple Michelin-starred restaurants. Baden-Baden's thermal baths, such as **Caracalla Spa (€19 for 2 hours)** and **Friedrichsbad (€35 for 3 hours)**, are perfect for relaxation after exploring.

Cultural & Historic Landmarks

**Heidelberg: Germany's Romantic Jewel**

- **Heidelberg Castle:** Open 8 AM – 6 PM, Entry €9
- **Philosophenweg (Philosopher's Walk):** Free, best visited at sunset
- **Old Bridge (Alte Brücke):** Iconic 18th-century landmark

Heidelberg, with its charming Old Town, is synonymous with romance and history. The stunning **Heidelberg Castle**, perched on a hill, offers breathtaking views of the Neckar River and the surrounding valley. The **Philosopher's Walk**, a scenic hillside path, is a must for panoramic views. Heidelberg is also home to Germany's oldest university, founded in 1386.

**Stuttgart: The Birthplace of Luxury Automobiles**
- **Mercedes-Benz Museum:** Open Tue-Sun, 9 AM – 6 PM, Entry €12
- **Porsche Museum:** Open Tue-Sun, 9 AM – 6 PM, Entry €10
- **Wilhelma Zoo & Botanical Garden:** Open daily, 8 AM – 6 PM, Entry €20

As the capital of Baden-Württemberg, Stuttgart is a modern city with a rich industrial heritage. It is home to two of the world's most famous automobile brands—Mercedes-Benz and Porsche. Their respective museums offer an in-depth look at automotive innovation, with stunning exhibits showcasing historic and futuristic designs.

Castles & Medieval Towns

**Hohenzollern Castle**
- **Opening Hours:** 10 AM – 5:30 PM
- **Entry Fee:** €22
- **Best Time to Visit:** Morning for fewer crowds

Germany is known for its castles, and **Hohenzollern Castle**, perched atop a mountain, is one of its most picturesque. This 19th-century neo-Gothic fortress offers panoramic views and a glimpse into Prussian royal history.

**Maulbronn Monastery (UNESCO Site)**
- **Opening Hours:** 9 AM – 5:30 PM
- **Entry Fee:** €9

This well-preserved medieval monastery is a UNESCO World Heritage Site and a masterpiece of Gothic and Romanesque architecture. It is one of Germany's most significant monastic sites and offers a peaceful retreat into history.

A Culinary Powerhouse

- **Must-Taste Dishes:** Maultaschen (Swabian Dumplings), Spätzle, Zwiebelrostbraten, Black Forest Cake
- **Best Michelin-Starred Restaurants:**
    - **Schwarzwaldstube (Baiersbronn)** – 3 Michelin stars
    - **Restaurant Ophelia (Konstanz)** – 2 Michelin stars
    - **Speisemeisterei (Stuttgart)** – 2 Michelin stars

Baden-Württemberg is Germany's culinary heartland. From hearty Swabian dishes to fine-dining experiences in Michelin-starred establishments, the region is a paradise for food lovers. The **Black Forest Cake**, a rich chocolate and cherry dessert, originates from this region and is a must-try.

Wine & Vineyards

- **Top Wine Regions:** Kaiserstuhl, Württemberg, Baden
- **Must-Try Wines:** Riesling, Lemberger, Trollinger

Baden-Württemberg is Germany's third-largest wine-producing region, specializing in **Rieslings** and **Pinot varieties**. A visit to **Kaiserstuhl** or **Württemberg** allows travelers to explore scenic vineyards and indulge in wine tastings at some of Germany's finest wineries.

## Brief History and Cultural Significance

### Origins and Early Civilizations

Baden-Württemberg, a region of deep historical roots, has been a cultural and strategic crossroads for millennia. The area was originally inhabited by Celtic tribes before the Romans arrived in the 1st century BCE, leaving behind extensive networks of roads, bathhouses, and fortifications, particularly in cities like Stuttgart and Heidelberg. The **Limes Germanicus**, a vast Roman frontier defense system stretching across the region, marked the boundary of the empire and shaped early settlements.

Following the decline of Rome, Germanic tribes, primarily the Alemanni, established dominance over the land. Their influence remains deeply embedded in the region's dialects, traditions, and folk practices. Charlemagne's conquest of the Alemanni in the 8th century integrated Baden-Württemberg into the Holy Roman Empire, setting the stage for its medieval development.

### The Rise of Principalities: Baden, Württemberg & Swabia

By the Middle Ages, Baden-Württemberg was not a unified entity but rather a collection of competing duchies, principalities, and bishoprics. The most influential were:

- **The Margraviate of Baden:** A territory that developed into the Grand Duchy of Baden, later becoming a key player in unifying southwestern Germany.
- **The Duchy of Württemberg:** A powerful Swabian state with Stuttgart as its capital, evolving into a kingdom in the 19th century.
- **The Free Imperial Cities:** Cities like Ulm, Heilbronn, and Esslingen held significant autonomy, flourishing through trade and commerce.

These fragmented states were at the heart of the Swabian League, a medieval alliance that sought to maintain stability and counter external threats. During the Protestant Reformation, Württemberg became a stronghold of Lutheranism, while Baden remained largely Catholic, further shaping the region's religious and cultural landscape.

## Industrialization and Economic Growth

The 19th century ushered in rapid modernization. Stuttgart became a hub of engineering and industry, laying the foundation for what would become global brands like **Mercedes-Benz and Porsche**. The Black Forest region, once reliant on agriculture and timber, saw an economic transformation with the rise of precision craftsmanship—most notably, the world-renowned **Black Forest cuckoo clocks**.

Educational institutions like the **University of Heidelberg** (founded in 1386, the oldest in Germany) attracted intellectuals and scholars, fostering innovation in science, philosophy, and literature. During this time, Baden-Württemberg became a cultural powerhouse, with figures like **Johann Friedrich von Schiller**, one of Germany's most revered poets and playwrights, leaving a lasting legacy.

## Baden-Württemberg and the Birth of Modern Germany

Baden-Württemberg played a crucial role in Germany's unification in 1871 under Prussian leadership. However, World War I and II deeply affected the region, with heavy bombing campaigns devastating cities like Stuttgart and Karlsruhe. After World War II, the region was divided into three separate states: Württemberg-Baden, Württemberg-Hohenzollern, and Baden, under French and American occupation.

In **1952, these states merged to form the modern state of Baden-Württemberg**, becoming one of Germany's most economically powerful and culturally rich regions. This merger brought together diverse traditions, blending Swabian, Baden, and Franconian influences into a unique regional identity.

## Cultural Significance and Heritage

Baden-Württemberg is a land where medieval heritage coexists with cutting-edge innovation. The region is home to **some of Germany's most picturesque castles**, including **Hohenzollern Castle, Lichtenstein Castle, and Heidelberg Castle**, each reflecting centuries of architectural evolution. The region also preserves its **folk traditions** through festivals like **Cannstatter Volksfest** (second only to Oktoberfest in size) and the historic **Swabian-Alemannic Fasnet**, a lively carnival rooted in medieval pagan customs.

In literature and philosophy, the influence of Baden-Württemberg extends far beyond its borders. **Hermann Hesse, the Nobel Prize-winning author of "Siddhartha" and "Steppenwolf,"** was born in Calw, while Friedrich Nietzsche, one of the most influential philosophers of the modern era, spent formative years in the region.

### A Region of Contrasts

Today, Baden-Württemberg balances **tradition and modernity**. The **Black Forest**, with its dense woodlands and tranquil villages, remains a stronghold of folklore and craftsmanship, while **Stuttgart and Karlsruhe** stand at the forefront of Germany's technological and automotive industries. The region's **wine culture** is among the finest in Europe, with world-class vineyards in **Heilbronn, Baden, and the Kaiserstuhl** producing some of Germany's best Riesling and Pinot Noir.

## Best Time to Visit

### Spring (March – June): A Season of Bloom and Festivals

Spring in Baden-Württemberg is one of the most visually stunning times to visit. The region awakens from winter's slumber, with cherry blossoms in Heidelberg, lush vineyards in Baden, and tulip gardens at **Mainau Island (Lake Constance, Opening Hours: 7:00 AM – 9:00 PM, Entry: €23.50 per adult, Free for children under 12)**.

### Why Visit in Spring?

- **Mild Weather:** Daytime temperatures range from 10°C in March to 20°C in May.

- **Fewer Crowds:** Attractions like **Hohenzollern Castle (Open daily 10:00 AM – 6:00 PM, Entry: €22 per adult)** are less crowded before summer.
- **Festival Season Begins:** The **Stuttgart Spring Festival (April–May)** is Europe's largest spring fair, featuring carnival rides and traditional beer tents.
- **Wine Country Awakens:** Vineyards in the Kaiserstuhl and Baden wine region begin hosting tastings.

**Ideal Activities in Spring:**
- Hike through the **Black Forest National Park (Entry: Free, Best Trails: Mummelsee & Wildsee)** while nature reawakens.
- Experience Swabian culture at **Esslingen Medieval Spring Market (Mid-April, Free Entry, Artisan Market & Costumed Performers)**.

**Summer (June – August): Peak Travel Season & Outdoor Escapes**

Summer is the busiest time in Baden-Württemberg, with long days (sunset at 10 PM) and warm temperatures (22–30°C). This is the season for outdoor adventure and festivals.

**Why Visit in Summer?**
- **Perfect for Lake Activities: Lake Constance (Strandbad Horn Beach, Open 9:00 AM – 8:00 PM, Entry: €4 per person)** is ideal for swimming and sailing.
- **Outdoor Castles & Palaces:** Explore **Lichtenstein Castle (Open 9:00 AM – 5:30 PM, Entry: €12 per adult, Guided Tours Available)**.
- **Summer Festivals:** The **Black Forest Open-Air Museum (Vogtsbauernhof, Open 9:00 AM – 6:00 PM, Entry: €10)** hosts folk festivals showcasing Swabian traditions.

**Challenges of Summer:**

- **Crowds & Higher Prices:** Hotels like **Brenners Park-Hotel & Spa in Baden-Baden (Starting at €450 per night, Michelin-star dining available)** are in high demand.
- **Heatwaves Possible:** Some years experience spikes of 35°C, making early morning or late evening sightseeing preferable.

## Autumn (September – October): Golden Vineyards & Ideal Hiking Weather

Autumn is arguably the **best season** to visit Baden-Württemberg. The summer crowds disappear, and the region's vineyards turn golden.

### Why Visit in Autumn?

- **Mild Weather:** 12–20°C with clear skies, ideal for hiking in the Swabian Jura and Black Forest.
- **Wine & Beer Festivals:** The **Stuttgart Wine Village (September, Free Entry, Wine Glass Rentals €5)** and **Cannstatter Volksfest (Late September – Early October, Beer Tents from €30 per seat)** celebrate local drinks and food.
- **Best Time for Photography: Heidelberg Castle (Open 8:00 AM – 6:00 PM, Entry: €9 per adult, Cable Car €7 extra)** is breathtaking against autumn foliage.

### Ideal Activities in Autumn:

- Take a scenic train ride on the **Schwäbische Alb Railway (Tickets: €10, Panoramic Views of Swabian Jura)**.
- Sample **Federweißer (new wine) and Zwiebelkuchen (onion tart)** at seasonal Weinfests.

## Winter (November – February): Christmas Magic & Thermal Spas

Winter is cold (0–5°C), but December is transformed by magical **Christmas markets. January and February are the best months for spa retreats.**

### Why Visit in Winter?

- **Christmas Markets:** **Stuttgart Christmas Market (Late November – December 23, Open 10:00 AM – 9:00 PM, Free Entry)** is one of Germany's oldest and most beautiful.
- **Thermal Spas:** Baden-Württemberg is famous for its wellness culture. Relax at **Caracalla Spa in Baden-Baden (Open 8:00 AM – 10:00 PM, Entry: €18 for 2 hours, Sauna Extra).**
- **Skiing & Snowboarding:** The **Black Forest Ski Resort Feldberg (Day Pass: €39, Equipment Rental Available)** offers well-groomed slopes.

**Ideal Winter Activities:**

- Take a **horse-drawn carriage ride in the Black Forest (Available in Triberg, €25 per person).**
- Enjoy Michelin-star dining at **Restaurant Schwarzwaldstube (Open 7:00 PM – 11:00 PM, Tasting Menu from €220).**

# CHAPTER 2.

# GETTING THERE

## International and Domestic Airports

### 1. Stuttgart Airport (Flughafen Stuttgart – STR)
- **Address:** Flughafenstraße 32, 70629 Stuttgart, Germany
- **Opening Hours:** 24/7 (Terminal services vary by airline)
- **Pricing:** No entry fee; parking rates range from €2 (short-term) to €25/day (long-term)
- **Key Airlines:** Lufthansa, Eurowings, KLM, Turkish Airlines, British Airways, Emirates
- **Facilities:** Duty-free shopping, lounges, restaurants, baggage services, car rentals
- **Transportation:** S-Bahn (S2, S3) to city center (€4.20, ~30 min), taxis (€35, ~25 min)

Stuttgart Airport is the largest and busiest airport in Baden-Württemberg, serving as the main gateway for both international and domestic travelers. Located about **13 km south** of Stuttgart's city center, it offers direct flights to **over 120 destinations worldwide**, including major European hubs like London, Paris, Amsterdam, and Istanbul, as well as long-haul routes via airlines like Emirates.

For passengers arriving from outside the Schengen zone, Stuttgart Airport has a well-organized customs and immigration process. Baggage claim is efficient, and transport connections to the city are seamless. The **S-Bahn S2 and S3 lines** run frequently, taking just **27 minutes to Stuttgart Hauptbahnhof (Main Station)**. Alternatively, taxis and private transfers are readily available outside Terminal 3, with fares averaging **€35–€45** depending on traffic.

Inside the terminal, travelers will find a variety of dining options, from quick snacks at **McDonald's (Terminal 3, Departure Level, 24/7)** to premium dining at **Top Air**, a Michelin-starred restaurant offering gourmet meals with a view of the runway. Shopping options include **Heinemann Duty-Free, Hugo Boss, and Porsche Design**, making it easy to pick up souvenirs or luxury items before departure.

For those in need of overnight stays, **Mövenpick Hotel Stuttgart Airport & Messe (★★★★, from €130/night)** is directly adjacent to the terminal, providing convenience and premium comfort. Budget travelers can opt for **Ibis Styles Stuttgart Airport Messe (★★★, from €85/night)**, which offers free shuttle service.

### 2. Karlsruhe/Baden-Baden Airport (FKB)

- **Address:** Victoria Boulevard A 106, 77836 Rheinmünster, Germany
- **Opening Hours:** 04:30 – 23:00 (Terminal services vary by flight schedule)
- **Pricing:** No entry fee; parking rates start at €1.50/hour, €8/day
- **Key Airlines:** Ryanair, Wizz Air, Corendon Airlines
- **Facilities:** Duty-free shopping, cafés, rental car services, free Wi-Fi
- **Transportation:** Bus 285 to Baden-Baden (€3.50, ~20 min), taxi (€35, ~15 min)

Karlsruhe/Baden-Baden Airport (FKB) is Baden-Württemberg's second-largest airport, specializing in **low-cost flights** across Europe. Located **40 km from Karlsruhe and 12 km from Baden-Baden**, this airport primarily serves Ryanair and Wizz Air routes, with flights to Spain, Italy, Greece, and Eastern Europe.

Although smaller than Stuttgart Airport, FKB is highly efficient, with **short waiting times at security and baggage claim**. Transportation to Baden-Baden's city center is easy via **Bus 285**, which departs every **30 minutes** and costs **€3.50** per ride. Taxis to Baden-Baden cost around **€35**, while direct shuttles to Karlsruhe are available for **€55**.

FKB has a limited but well-curated selection of shops and restaurants. The **Duty-Free store** offers tax-free goods, while **Bistro Bel Air** serves quick German-style meals. Travelers seeking accommodations nearby can book the **Hotel Zum Schwan (★★★, from €70/night, 3 km away)** or opt for luxury at **Brenners Park-Hotel & Spa (★★★★★, from €290/night, Baden-Baden)**.

### 3. Friedrichshafen Airport (Bodensee-Airport – FDH)

- **Address:** Am Flugplatz 64, 88046 Friedrichshafen, Germany
- **Opening Hours:** 06:00 – 23:00
- **Pricing:** Parking from €2/hour, €15/day
- **Key Airlines:** Lufthansa, British Airways, SunExpress
- **Facilities:** Airport lounge, rental cars, café, business center
- **Transportation:** Bus 7586 to Friedrichshafen (€3, ~15 min), train (€4.50, ~20 min)

Located **on the northern shore of Lake Constance**, Friedrichshafen Airport is ideal for visitors heading to **Bodensee, Lindau, and the Allgäu region**. While smaller than STR and FKB, it offers essential European connections, particularly to **Munich, Frankfurt, and Vienna** via Lufthansa.

One of FDH's standout features is the **Zeppelin Museum**, located just **4 km from the terminal**, where visitors can learn about the region's aviation history. The airport itself is **compact and hassle-free**, with quick security checks and short walking distances between gates.

Traveling from the airport to Friedrichshafen is easy via **Bus 7586**, which departs every **30 minutes** and costs **€3**. A direct train to **Lindau Hauptbahnhof** is also available, taking **20 minutes** and costing **€4.50**.

For dining, travelers can grab a meal at **Flyer's Lounge Café**, which serves fresh pastries and coffee. Nearby hotels include the **Comfort Hotel Friedrichshafen (★★★, from €85/night, 2 km away)** and the luxurious **Hotel Bad Schachen (★★★★★, from €210/night, Lindau)**.

### 4. Mannheim City Airport (MHG) – Regional Business Hub

- **Address:** Seckenheimer Landstraße 170, 68163 Mannheim, Germany
- **Opening Hours:** 05:30 – 22:00
- **Pricing:** Parking starts at €1.50/hour, €12/day
- **Key Airlines:** Rhein-Neckar Air, Private Charters
- **Facilities:** Executive lounge, rental cars, business terminal
- **Transportation:** Tram Line 5 to Mannheim Hbf (€2.80, ~15 min), taxi (€20, ~10 min)

Mannheim City Airport primarily serves **business travelers** with domestic flights to Berlin, Hamburg, and Sylt. It is a convenient alternative for those traveling to the **Rhine-Neckar metropolitan region**. While small, it features an executive lounge and seamless **check-in services for private charters**.

A highlight of MHG is its **proximity to Heidelberg**, which is just **15 km away**. Travelers can take a direct tram from the airport to **Mannheim Hauptbahnhof (Main Station)** and transfer to Heidelberg in **under 30 minutes**.

Nearby hotels include **NH Mannheim (★★★★, from €95/night, 3 km away)** and the elegant **Hotel Europäischer Hof Heidelberg (★★★★★, from €250/night, Heidelberg)**.

## Train and Bus Connections

**1. Train Travel in Baden-Württemberg**

Baden-Württemberg is exceptionally well-connected by Germany's **Deutsche Bahn (DB)** rail network, providing efficient and comfortable train services to major cities, historic towns, and scenic regions. The state also has its **own regional railway systems**, including the S-Bahn and local trains.

**Key Train Stations & Connections**

- **Stuttgart Hauptbahnhof (Main Station)**
    - **Address:** Arnulf-Klett-Platz 2, 70173 Stuttgart
    - **Opening Hours:** 24/7 (Ticket counters: 06:00–22:00)
    - **Pricing:** Regional tickets start at €19; long-distance trains vary (€29–€99)
    - **Connections:** ICE/IC high-speed trains to Munich, Frankfurt, and Berlin; regional trains to Black Forest, Heidelberg, Freiburg
    - **Facilities:** Luggage storage, restrooms, shopping, dining, and lounges
- **Karlsruhe Hauptbahnhof**
    - **Address:** Bahnhofplatz 1, 76137 Karlsruhe
    - **Opening Hours:** 24/7 (Ticket counters: 06:00–22:00)
    - **Pricing:** Regional tickets from €17, long-distance from €29

- - - Connections:** Key hub for Baden region; direct trains to Stuttgart, Frankfurt, and Basel (Switzerland)
- **Freiburg Hauptbahnhof**
    - **Address:** Bismarckallee 5-7, 79098 Freiburg
    - **Opening Hours:** 24/7 (Ticket counters: 06:00–22:00)
    - **Pricing:** Regional from €19, ICE tickets from €29
    - **Connections:** Gateway to the Black Forest; direct trains to Stuttgart, Basel, and Munich

**Types of Train Services**

- **ICE (InterCity Express):** High-speed trains connecting major German and European cities (e.g., Stuttgart to Berlin in ~5 hours).
- **IC (InterCity):** Slower than ICE but still fast, connecting cities like Mannheim, Ulm, and Heidelberg.
- **IRE (Interregio-Express):** Fast regional trains with fewer stops, ideal for travel within Baden-Württemberg.
- **RE (Regional-Express) & RB (Regionalbahn):** Local trains connecting towns and villages to major hubs.
- **S-Bahn (Suburban Trains):** Covers urban areas like Stuttgart, Karlsruhe, and Mannheim.

**Train Passes & Ticketing**

- **Baden-Württemberg Ticket (€26 for 1 person, +€8 per extra traveler)**
    - Unlimited travel for a day on regional trains, trams, and buses.
    - Valid from 09:00–03:00 the next day (weekdays) and all day on weekends.
- **Deutschland Ticket (€49/month)**

- - Unlimited travel across Germany on all regional trains, trams, and buses.
- **Super Sparpreis & Sparpreis Tickets**
  - Discounted tickets for ICE/IC trains when booked in advance (from €19.90).

**Train Travel Tips**

- **Reservations** are required for ICE and IC trains but not for regional services.
- **Luggage storage** is available at major stations (€3–€6 per locker).
- **Bikes** can be taken on regional trains with a Fahrradkarte (€5–€9).

## 2. Bus Travel in Baden-Württemberg

Buses in Baden-Württemberg complement train services, covering areas that lack rail connections, especially rural villages and nature parks.

### Key Long-Distance Bus Stations & Connections

- **Stuttgart ZOB (Central Bus Station)**
  - **Address:** Suttgart Airport Busterminal, Flughafenstr. 61, 70629 Stuttgart
  - **Opening Hours:** 24/7 (ticket counters: 06:00–22:00)
  - **Pricing:** FlixBus fares start at €5 for short trips, €15–€30 for long routes
  - **Connections:** Munich, Frankfurt, Zurich, Paris
- **Karlsruhe Bus Station**
  - **Address:** Hinterm Hauptbahnhof 6, 76137 Karlsruhe
  - **Opening Hours:** 06:00–22:00

- **Pricing:** FlixBus and Blablacar Bus from €7–€25
- **Connections:** Direct routes to Frankfurt, Basel, Strasbourg

**Types of Bus Services**

- **Long-Distance Buses (FlixBus, BlaBlaCar Bus, IC Bus)**
  - Budget-friendly alternative to trains for intercity and international travel.
  - Popular routes: Stuttgart to Munich (~3 hours), Freiburg to Zurich (~2 hours).
- **Regional Buses (RVS, SWEG, SBG)**
  - Connect small towns and rural areas with train stations.
  - Key lines serve the Black Forest, Swabian Jura, and Lake Constance.
- **City Buses**
  - Operated by local transport authorities (e.g., VVS in Stuttgart, VRN in Mannheim).
  - Frequent and well-integrated with tram and S-Bahn services.

**Bus Ticketing & Passes**

- **Single Ride Tickets (€2.50–€3.50)**
  - Varies by city and distance.
- **Day Passes (€5–€9 per city, €20+ for regional travel)**
  - Unlimited bus, tram, and S-Bahn rides for one day.
- **Kombitickets**
  - Many attractions (e.g., Europa Park, Heidelberg Castle) offer combined entry and transport tickets.

**Bus Travel Tips**

- **Buying Tickets:** Available via mobile apps (DB Navigator, FlixBus), ticket machines, or on board (cash/card).
- **Punctuality:** Regional buses often run on time but may be delayed in rural areas.
- **Luggage Policy:** Large suitcases are allowed on long-distance buses but not always on city buses.

## Driving Routes and Car Rentals

**Driving Routes to Baden-Württemberg**

Baden-Württemberg is well connected to Germany's autobahn network, making it easily accessible by car from various parts of Europe. Below are key driving routes:

**From Frankfurt (Approx. 1.5 – 2.5 Hours)**

- **Route:** Take the A5 south towards Karlsruhe or the A67/A6 towards Stuttgart.
- **Best For:** Quick access to northern Baden-Württemberg cities like Heidelberg, Mannheim, and Karlsruhe.
- **Attractions Along the Way:** Bergstraße Wine Route, Schwetzingen Palace.

**From Munich (Approx. 2 – 3.5 Hours)**

- **Route:** Take the A8 west towards Stuttgart or the A96 towards Lake Constance.
- **Best For:** Those heading to Stuttgart, Ulm, or the southwestern lakeside areas.
- **Attractions Along the Way:** Ulm Minster, Blautopf Spring.

**From Zurich (Approx. 1.5 – 3 Hours)**

- **Route:** Take the A1/A4 to the German border at Konstanz or the A81 to Stuttgart.
- **Best For:** Travelers heading to Lake Constance or the Black Forest region.
- **Attractions Along the Way:** Rhine Falls in Schaffhausen, Mainau Island.

**From Strasbourg (Approx. 1 – 2.5 Hours)**

- **Route:** Take the A5 north towards Baden-Baden or A35/A8 towards Stuttgart.
- **Best For:** Entering Baden-Württemberg via the scenic Upper Rhine Valley.
- **Attractions Along the Way:** Black Forest National Park, Baden-Baden's Thermal Spas.

**From Paris (Approx. 5 – 6 Hours)**

- **Route:** Take the A4 towards Strasbourg, then A5/A8 into Baden-Württemberg.
- **Best For:** A road trip from France with stops in Alsace before entering Germany.
- **Attractions Along the Way:** Alsatian wine villages, Heidelberg Castle.

**Car Rentals in Baden-Württemberg**

Renting a car is an excellent option for flexibility, especially when visiting remote locations like the Black Forest or small wine villages.

**Car Rental Locations & Operating Hours**

1. **Stuttgart Airport (STR) – Car Rental Center**
    - **Address:** Flughafenstr. 43, 70629 Stuttgart, Germany
    - **Opening Hours:** 06:00 – 23:30 (Varies by provider)

- Pricing: From €40/day for economy cars, luxury vehicles €100+
- Key Providers: Sixt, Europcar, Hertz, Avis, Enterprise

2. **Frankfurt Airport (FRA) – Car Rental Center**
    - **Address:** Terminal 1 & 2, Hugo-Eckener-Ring, 60549 Frankfurt
    - **Opening Hours:** 24/7 service available
    - **Pricing:** From €35/day, discounts for weekly rentals
    - **Key Providers:** Sixt, Europcar, Budget, Alamo

3. **Freiburg Hauptbahnhof – Train Station Rentals**
    - **Address:** Bismarckallee 7F, 79098 Freiburg
    - **Opening Hours:** 07:00 – 20:00 (Varies by company)
    - **Pricing:** From €45/day
    - **Key Providers:** Hertz, Buchbinder, Europcar

4. **Karlsruhe Downtown – City Rental Offices**
    - **Address:** Kriegsstraße 90, 76133 Karlsruhe
    - **Opening Hours:** 08:00 – 18:00
    - **Pricing:** Compact cars from €39/day, SUVs from €65/day
    - **Key Providers:** Enterprise, Avis, Flizzr

**Rental Requirements & Policies**

- **Minimum Age:** 21 years (Some companies require 25+ for premium vehicles)
- **License:** EU driver's license or International Driving Permit (IDP) for non-EU visitors
- **Deposit:** Typically €500 – €1,500 held on a credit card

- **Insurance:** Third-party liability included; CDW (Collision Damage Waiver) recommended
- **One-Way Rentals:** Available for an extra fee, useful for dropping off in another city

## Visa and Entry Requirements

**Visa & Entry Overview**
- **Address:** Federal Foreign Office, Werderscher Markt 1, 10117 Berlin, Germany
- **Opening Times:** Monday to Friday, 9:00 AM – 5:00 PM
- **Pricing:** Varies by visa type; Schengen visa standard fee is **€80 for adults, €40 for children (6-12 years), free for children under 6**
- **Processing Time:** Typically **15 calendar days**, but can extend up to **45 days** in exceptional cases

**Who Needs a Visa to Enter Baden-Württemberg, Germany?**

Baden-Württemberg is part of Germany and follows **Schengen Area** entry regulations. **EU/EEA/Swiss nationals** can enter freely without a visa. **Non-EU travelers** fall into two categories:

1. **Visa-Exempt Countries** – Stays up to **90 days within 180 days**:
   - U.S., Canada, UK, Australia, New Zealand, Japan, South Korea, UAE, and several others.
   - Passport must be valid **at least 3 months beyond departure**.
2. **Visa-Required Countries** – Stays over **90 days OR from restricted nations**:

- Citizens from India, China, Russia, Philippines, South Africa, and others must apply for a **Schengen Visa** before arrival.

**Types of Visas for Travelers to Baden-Württemberg**

**1. Schengen Tourist Visa (Short Stay – Type C)**

- For tourism, visiting family/friends, or short business trips
- Allows up to **90 days** within **180 days**
- Single, double, or multiple-entry options

**Requirements:**

- Completed **Schengen Visa Application Form**
- **Valid passport** (issued in the last **10 years** and valid **3 months beyond departure**)
- Two **biometric passport photos** (recent, 35x45 mm)
- **Travel itinerary**: Round-trip flight reservation or travel bookings
- **Proof of accommodation**: Hotel bookings, Airbnb confirmation, or invitation letter from a host
- **Financial proof**: Bank statements (last 3-6 months), payslips, or sponsorship letter
- **Travel insurance**: Minimum **€30,000 medical coverage**, valid for all Schengen states
- **Visa fee**: €80 (standard), €40 (children 6-12), free for children under 6

**2. National Visa (Long Stay – Type D)**

- Required for **stays exceeding 90 days** (study, work, business, family reunification)
- Application must be made **at a German consulate/embassy** in home country

**Where to Apply?**
- **At the German Embassy or Consulate** in your country
- **Visa Application Centers (VACs)** such as **VFS Global** or **TLScontact** (for certain regions)

Entry at the Border – Documents & Screening

Even with a visa exemption, border control may ask for:
- **Return ticket** proving intention to leave before 90 days expire
- **Proof of funds** (approx. **€45 per day** per person)
- **Accommodation confirmation**
- **Travel insurance proof**

**Denial & Reapplication**

If rejected, applicants receive a **written explanation**. Reapplication is possible after **correcting the reasons for refusal** (e.g., insufficient funds, missing documents). Appeals must be filed within **one month** of rejection.

**Visa Extensions in Germany**

Short-stay visas **cannot be extended** except for:
- **Force majeure** (e.g., flight cancellations, medical emergencies)
- **Humanitarian reasons**

# CHAPTER 3.

# LOCAL TRANSPORTATION

## Public Transport: Trams, Buses & Trains

1. Trains (Regionalbahn, Regional Express & S-Bahn)
   - S-Bahn (Suburban Rail):
     - Major cities such as Stuttgart, Mannheim, and Karlsruhe have extensive **S-Bahn networks**.
     - **Operating Hours:** Generally 4:30 AM – 1:00 AM; some lines offer weekend night services.
     - **Frequency:** Every 10–20 minutes in cities, 30–60 minutes in rural areas.
   - Regionalbahn (RB) & Regional Express (RE):
     - Connects smaller towns and rural areas with major hubs.
     - Slower than long-distance IC/ICE trains but more affordable.
     - **Key routes:**
       - Stuttgart ⇆ Heidelberg ⇆ Mannheim
       - Freiburg ⇆ Offenburg ⇆ Karlsruhe
       - Ulm ⇆ Tübingen ⇆ Reutlingen

**Important Tip:** Always check whether your ticket is valid for long-distance **IC/ICE trains**, as some regional tickets only cover RE, RB, and S-Bahn services.

## 2. Trams (Straßenbahn)

Trams are the backbone of city transport in **Stuttgart, Karlsruhe, Freiburg, Mannheim, and Heidelberg**, offering frequent connections within urban centers.

- **Operating Hours:** Typically 5:00 AM – 12:30 AM.
- **Frequency:** Every 5–15 minutes depending on the time of day.
- **Notable Tram Systems:**
    - **Karlsruhe's Tram-Train Network (AVG):** One of the most advanced in the world, allowing trams to run on both city tracks and regional railway lines.
    - **Freiburg's Green Trams:** The city has a fully electric and eco-friendly tram network.

**Recommended Route:** Take **Tram Line 5 in Freiburg** for a scenic ride through the historic center.

## 3. Buses

Buses fill transport gaps where trains and trams don't operate, particularly in smaller towns and rural areas.

- **City Buses:** Operate frequently, running every 10–20 minutes during peak hours.
- **Rural & Regional Buses:** Less frequent (every 30–60 minutes), often connecting with train stations.
- **Night Buses:** Available in major cities like Stuttgart, Mannheim, and Freiburg, typically operating from **midnight to 5:00 AM** on weekends.

**Tip:** Some regional buses offer **"Rufbus"** (on-demand bus services), requiring reservations in advance.

## 4. Funiculars & Special Transport

Baden-Württemberg features some **historic funiculars and mountain railways**, offering both practical transport and scenic experiences:

- **Heidelberg's Königstuhl Funicular** (Station: Kornmarkt) – Operates daily from **9:00 AM – 5:00 PM** (€14 round-trip).
- **Stuttgart's Standseilbahn (Forest Cemetery Funicular)** – A charming historic railway connecting Südheimer Platz to the forested cemetery area.
- **Merkur Bergbahn in Baden-Baden** – Germany's longest funicular, reaching the Merkur Mountain summit.

### Accessibility & Travel Tips

- **Wheelchair Accessibility:** Major stations and transport hubs have elevators and ramps. Most trams and buses are **low-floor** for easy boarding.
- **Bike Transport:** Bicycles are allowed on **regional trains and some S-Bahn lines**, usually outside peak hours. Look for compartments marked with a bicycle symbol.
- **Punctuality:** While German trains are known for precision, **regional delays (5–15 minutes) are common**, particularly in winter months. Always check real-time schedules on **DB Navigator** or local transport apps.

## Car Rentals and Driving Tips

### Car Rental Locations, Opening Hours & Pricing

Baden-Württemberg has numerous car rental agencies available at airports, city centers, and major train stations. Below are key locations, their operating hours, and general pricing details:

**Major Car Rental Locations**
- **Stuttgart Airport (STR) – Car Rental Center**
    - **Address:** Flughafenstraße 43, 70629 Stuttgart, Germany
    - **Opening Hours:** 06:00 – 23:30 (Daily)
    - **Pricing:** Economy cars from €45/day, SUVs from €70/day, luxury cars from €120/day
- **Heidelberg Central Station – Rental Desk**
    - **Address:** Willy-Brandt-Platz 5, 69115 Heidelberg, Germany
    - **Opening Hours:** 07:00 – 21:00 (Monday-Saturday), 08:00 – 18:00 (Sunday)
    - **Pricing:** Compact cars from €50/day, vans from €90/day
- **Freiburg Downtown – Europcar & Sixt**
    - **Address:** Bismarckallee 7, 79098 Freiburg, Germany
    - **Opening Hours:** 08:00 – 19:00 (Monday-Saturday), Closed Sunday
    - **Pricing:** Mid-size cars from €60/day, electric vehicles from €75/day
- **Ulm – Main Train Station Rental Services**
    - **Address:** Bahnhofplatz 1, 89073 Ulm, Germany
    - **Opening Hours:** 07:30 – 20:00 (Daily)
    - **Pricing:** Compact cars from €55/day, luxury sedans from €110/day

**Important Car Rental Policies**

- **Minimum Age Requirement:** Most companies require drivers to be at least **21 years old** (some premium cars require 25+).
- **License Requirement:** A **valid EU/EEA driver's license** is required. Non-EU tourists need an **International Driving Permit (IDP)** alongside their home license.
- **Deposit & Insurance:** Expect a deposit of €500–€1500, depending on car type. Insurance options include **Collision Damage Waiver (CDW)** and **Liability Insurance** (recommended).

**Driving Tips in Baden-Württemberg**

**1. Understanding Road Types & Speed Limits**

- **Autobahn (A-Routes):** No official speed limit on some sections, but **130 km/h is the recommended max speed**. Watch for restricted zones where limits apply.
- **Bundesstraßen (B-Routes):** Federal roads with **100 km/h** limits unless signposted otherwise.
- **Urban Areas:** Speed limit is **50 km/h**, reduced to **30 km/h** in residential zones.
- **Rural & Mountain Roads:** Expect **70–100 km/h** limits and sharp curves, especially in the Black Forest region.

**2. Navigating Traffic Rules & Road Signs**

- **Priority to the Right:** In the absence of traffic lights or signs, vehicles coming from the right always have priority.
- **Flashing Green Light at Traffic Signals:** Unlike some countries, a flashing green means the signal is about to turn red, so prepare to stop.

- **No Right Turn on Red:** Unlike in the U.S., turning right on a red light is strictly prohibited unless indicated by a green arrow sign.
- **Low Emission Zones (Umweltzonen):** Cities like Stuttgart, Heidelberg, and Freiburg require vehicles to have an **emission sticker (Umweltplakette)** to enter. Rental companies typically provide compliant cars, but verify before renting.

### 3. Parking Guidelines & Costs

- **City Center Parking:**
    - Street parking is limited and costs **€2–€4 per hour**.
    - Use **"P+R" (Park and Ride)** facilities on the outskirts to avoid high fees.
- **Hotel Parking:**
    - Many luxury and mid-range hotels charge **€15–€25 per night** for private parking.
- **Black Forest & Rural Parking:**
    - Parking at hiking trails or nature sites often costs **€3–€5 for the day** via ticket machines.
    - Free parking is available in smaller villages.

### 4. Fuel Stations & Electric Charging Points

- **Fuel Types & Costs:**
    - **Diesel (Diesel):** ~€1.80/liter
    - **Unleaded Petrol (Super E5):** ~€1.95/liter
    - **Super Plus (High-Octane):** ~€2.10/liter
- **24/7 Fuel Stations:** Available along highways (Autobahn) and major cities, but rural areas may have limited hours.
- **EV Charging:** Over **1,500 charging points** in Stuttgart alone; major hubs include:

- Karlsruhe Central Station EV Hub (€0.39/kWh)
- Stuttgart Königstraße Fast Chargers (€0.45/kWh)
- Freiburg Solar-Powered Stations (€0.35/kWh)

## 5. Scenic Driving Routes & Road Conditions

- **Black Forest High Road (B500):** One of Germany's most famous scenic drives, stretching **60 km** from Baden-Baden to Freudenstadt. Expect **breathtaking mountain views**, well-paved roads, and ample scenic stops.
- **Swabian Alb Route:** Runs through **castles, vineyards, and prehistoric caves**, with well-maintained roads but steep inclines.
- **Lake Constance Coastal Drive:** Stunning lakeside route but often **crowded in summer**. Drive early in the morning to avoid congestion.
- **Hohenzollern Castle Drive:** Winding roads through lush countryside, ideal for renting a convertible.

## 6. Winter Driving Precautions

- **Winter Tires Mandatory (Nov – April):** Snow-covered roads in the Black Forest and Swabian Jura require proper winter tires. Rental agencies equip cars accordingly, but double-check before booking.
- **Black Ice & Snow Chains:**
    - Roads in higher altitudes can be **icy, even in March**. Drive slowly in mountain areas.
    - Snow chains are **recommended** for extreme winter conditions, particularly near ski resorts.

## 7. Border Crossings & International Travel

- **Crossing into Switzerland, France & Austria:**

- Rentals usually allow cross-border travel but inform the agency in advance.
- **Switzerland:** Must purchase a **Vignette** (€40) for highway access.
- **Austria:** Requires a **motorway toll sticker (Pickerl)** for €9.90 (10-day validity).
- **Returning the Car in a Different Country:** Some companies charge a **€100–€300** one-way rental fee for returning cars outside Germany.

## Biking and Walking Routes

1. **Schwarzwald Panorama Cycle Route (Black Forest)**
    - **Starting Point:** Pforzheim, Baden-Württemberg
    - **Ending Point:** Waldshut-Tiengen, near the Swiss border
    - **Opening Times:** Open year-round, best from April to October
    - **Pricing:** Free access; bike rentals range from €15-€40 per day
    - **Bike Rental & Services:**
        - Rad + Tat, Pforzheim (€18/day, e-bikes available)
        - Fahrradverleih Freiburg (€20/day, guided tours optional)
    - **Nearby Dining:**
        - **Restaurant Zum Wilden Michel** (Traditional Black Forest cuisine, Pforzheim)

- - **Hausbrauerei Feierling** (Local brewery, Freiburg)
  - **Recommended Accommodation:**
    - **Parkhotel Pforzheim** (Luxury, €150/night)
    - **Hotel Schwarzwaldhof, Titisee** (Mid-range, €90/night)

2. **Lake Constance Cycle Path (Bodensee-Radweg)**
   - **Starting Point:** Konstanz, Baden-Württemberg
   - **Route Covers:** Konstanz, Meersburg, Friedrichshafen, Lindau
   - **Opening Times:** Open year-round, peak season from May to September
   - **Pricing:** Free access; rentals from €15-€35 per day
   - **Bike Rental & Services:**
     - **Radhaus Konstanz** (€18/day, child seats available)
     - **Radverleih Meersburg** (€22/day, e-bikes €35)
   - **Nearby Dining:**
     - **Weinstube Birnauer Oberhof** (Lakeview wine bar, Meersburg)
     - **Al Porto Café, Konstanz** (Casual dining, local fish dishes)
   - **Recommended Accommodation:**
     - **Steigenberger Inselhotel, Konstanz** (Luxury, €180/night)
     - **Seehotel Friedrichshafen** (Mid-range, €100/night)

3. **Stuttgart City Walking & Cycling Routes**
    - **Starting Point:** Schlossplatz, Stuttgart
    - **Key Landmarks:** Königstraße, Mercedes-Benz Museum, Wilhelma Zoo
    - **Opening Times:** Public access 24/7; museums have varied hours
    - **Pricing:** Free to walk/bike; museum entries vary (€10-€15)
    - **Bike Rental & Services:**
        - **RegioRadStuttgart** (€1/30 min, e-bikes available)
    - **Nearby Dining:**
        - **Stuttgarter Stäffele** (Authentic Swabian food, Königstraße)
        - **Cube Restaurant** (Fine dining with city views)
    - **Recommended Accommodation:**
        - **Althoff Hotel am Schlossgarten** (€160/night)
        - **Motel One Stuttgart-Hauptbahnhof** (€80/night)

**Top Biking and Walking Routes in Baden-Württemberg**

**1. Schwarzwald Panorama Cycle Route (Black Forest)**

This 280 km long-distance cycling route traverses the breathtaking Black Forest, offering panoramic views of valleys, dense woodlands, and historic towns. It is well-paved, making it ideal for both seasoned cyclists and e-bike users. Riders pass through charming spa towns like Bad Wildbad and picturesque villages such as Triberg, home to Germany's highest waterfall. The climb near Feldberg (the region's highest peak) is challenging but rewarding with spectacular scenery.

## 2. Lake Constance Cycle Path (Bodensee-Radweg)

Encircling Lake Constance, this 260 km route offers a mix of lakeside serenity, vineyard landscapes, and historical towns. The stretch from Meersburg to Lindau is particularly scenic, with ferry crossings allowing cyclists to customize their journey. The relatively flat terrain makes it perfect for casual cyclists. Stop at Mainau Island for its famous flower gardens or Friedrichshafen for Zeppelin history.

## 3. Heidelberg Philosophenweg Walking Trail

One of Germany's most scenic urban walking routes, this 2 km trail in Heidelberg offers stunning views of the Old Town, the Neckar River, and Heidelberg Castle. The path was historically used by philosophers and poets for inspiration. It includes shaded gardens, historic ruins, and hidden benches for relaxation. It's accessible but steep in some areas.

## 4. Stuttgart's Stäffele Walking Route

Stuttgart is famous for its "Stäffele" (historic stairways), which climb through vineyards, gardens, and old neighborhoods. The Stäffele walk takes visitors from Schlossplatz to Karlshöhe and continues up to Weissenburgpark, offering rewarding panoramic views. It's a mix of cobbled paths, lush parks, and historical sites, making it a unique way to explore Stuttgart on foot.

## 5. Swabian Alps Cycling Trail (Alb-Crossing)

Covering 370 km, this route runs from Aalen to Tuttlingen, crossing the Swabian Jura, a region known for its limestone cliffs, caves, and prehistoric sites. The ride takes you through UNESCO-listed caves where Ice Age artifacts were found. Highlights include Hohenzollern Castle and the dramatic rock formations of the Danube Valley.

## 6. Freiburg to Schauinsland Mountain Route

This 18 km uphill cycling route from Freiburg leads to Schauinsland, offering one of the best panoramic views of the Black Forest. The road is steep but paved, and cyclists can take a cable car down for an easier return. Along the way, there are scenic picnic spots and traditional mountain huts serving hearty local dishes like Käsespätzle.

### 7. Bad Wimpfen & Neckar Valley Walking Route

A picturesque 12 km riverside walk from Bad Wimpfen to Gundelsheim, passing medieval castles, vineyards, and traditional half-timbered houses. The route follows the Neckar River and includes stops at scenic overlooks, local wineries, and historical sites like the Blue Tower in Bad Wimpfen.

### Practical Tips for Biking & Walking in Baden-Württemberg

- **Best Time for Biking & Walking:** Spring (April-June) and Fall (September-October) offer mild weather, fewer crowds, and stunning landscapes.
- **Bike Rental Options:** Most cities have short-term rentals, while long-distance riders can find multi-day bike hire services.
- **Signage & Path Quality:** All major routes are well-marked with signage and rest stops, making navigation easy.
- **Packing Essentials:** Bring water, sunscreen, and rain protection, especially for mountain routes.
- **Public Transport & Bike Transfers:** Deutsche Bahn trains allow bike transport, with designated carriages on most regional trains.

## Taxi and Ride-Sharing Services

### Taxis in Baden-Württemberg

Taxis are a reliable mode of transport across cities like Stuttgart, Karlsruhe, Mannheim, and Freiburg. They are regulated, metered, and ensure a safe, predictable journey.

**Taxi Stands & Availability**
- Found at airports, train stations, major hotels, and city centers
- Well-marked with clear signage
- Available 24/7 in urban areas, though less frequent in smaller towns at night

**Pricing Structure**
- **Base Fare**: €3.50 – €4.50 (varies by city)
- **Per Kilometer**: €1.80 – €2.50
- **Waiting Time**: €35 – €50 per hour
- **Extra Charges**: Late-night (usually +10%), luggage fees, and pre-booking fees

**Top Taxi Companies by City**
- **Stuttgart**: Stuttgarter Taxi AG (+49 711 19410)
- **Freiburg**: Taxi Freiburg (+49 761 55555)
- **Mannheim**: Taxi Mannheim (+49 621 444044)
- **Karlsruhe**: Taxi Karlsruhe (+49 721 944144)

**Booking Options**
- **Phone Call**: Available in all cities, but expect German-speaking operators
- **App-Based**: FREE NOW (formerly mytaxi) is the most popular option
- **Street Hailing**: Possible in city centers but rare in suburban areas

**Airport & Hotel Transfers**
- Fixed-rate transfers from Stuttgart Airport to city center (€40–€50)
- Many hotels offer private taxi arrangements for guests

**Ride-Sharing Services**

While taxis are dominant, ride-sharing apps are increasingly popular in Baden-Württemberg. Uber, Bolt, and BlaBlaCar operate in major cities, offering convenient, cashless rides.

**Uber**

- **Available in**: Stuttgart, Mannheim, Karlsruhe, Freiburg
- **Ride Options**: UberX (standard), UberBlack (luxury), UberXL (larger groups)
- **Pricing**: Dynamic based on demand; usually 10–20% cheaper than taxis
- **Booking**: Via the Uber app only
- **Payment**: Cashless (card or mobile payment)

**Bolt**

- **Available in**: Stuttgart and Mannheim (limited coverage)
- **Cheaper alternative to Uber** with competitive fares
- **App-based only**, similar pricing model to Uber

**BlaBlaCar (Long-Distance Ride-Sharing)**

- **Best for intercity travel** between Baden-Württemberg's towns and Germany-wide
- **Drivers offer seats** in their private cars for pre-set fares
- **Example Route Pricing**:
    - Stuttgart to Heidelberg: ~€10
    - Freiburg to Karlsruhe: ~€12
    - Stuttgart to Munich: ~€20
- **Booking**: Via the BlaBlaCar website or app

**MOIA (Stuttgart & Hannover Only)**

- **Electric ride-sharing service** with multiple passengers per ride

- **Operates via app**, with pick-up points similar to bus stops
- **More eco-friendly and affordable** than taxis or Uber

**Tips for Using Taxis & Ride-Sharing in Baden-Württemberg**

1. **For Late-Night Travel**: Book in advance, as availability can be low outside Stuttgart and Mannheim.
2. **For Airports & Train Stations**: Use official taxi stands to avoid unlicensed operators.
3. **For the Cheapest Ride**: Compare Uber and Bolt prices before booking.
4. **For Rural Areas**: Taxis are often the only option, and pre-booking is recommended.
5. **For Group Travel**: Consider BlaBlaCar for affordable intercity trips.
6. **For Eco-Conscious Travel**: MOIA is a greener alternative in Stuttgart.

# CHAPTER 4.

# ACCOMMODATION OPTIONS

## Luxury Hotels and Resorts

**1. Brenners Park-Hotel & Spa (Baden-Baden)**

📍 **Address:** Schillerstraße 4/6, 76530 Baden-Baden, Germany; **Check-in:** From 3:00 PM | **Check-out:** Until 12:00 PM; 💰 **Pricing:** Starting at €500 per night; 🍽 **Dining:** Fritz & Felix (modern European cuisine), Wintergarten (elegant fine dining), Kaminhalle (afternoon tea and cocktails)

Why Stay Here?

Brenners Park-Hotel & Spa is a legendary five-star retreat in Baden-Baden, known for its opulence and history of hosting royalty and celebrities. Overlooking the Lichtentaler Allee park, this grand hotel combines Belle Époque architecture with state-of-the-art spa facilities.

**Key Features:**

- **Villa Stéphanie Spa & Wellbeing:** A 5,000 sqm wellness center offering medical spa treatments, hydrotherapy, and digital detox programs.
- **Elegant Rooms & Suites:** Spacious accommodations with marble bathrooms, antique furnishings, and private terraces.

- **Close to Attractions:** Walking distance from the famous Friedrichsbad and Caracalla Spa.

## 2. Hotel Traube Tonbach (Black Forest)

**Address:** Tonbachstraße 237, 72270 Baiersbronn, Germany; **Check-in:** From 3:00 PM | **Check-out:** Until 11:00 AM; **Pricing:** Starting at €450 per night; **Dining:** Schwarzwaldstube (Michelin-starred fine dining), 1789 (traditional Swabian cuisine), Silberberg (international buffet)

Why Stay Here?

Hotel Traube Tonbach is a family-run, five-star establishment in the heart of the Black Forest, renowned for its exceptional hospitality and culinary excellence.

**Key Features:**

- **Culinary Excellence:** Home to Schwarzwaldstube, one of Germany's most famous Michelin-starred restaurants.
- **Luxury Wellness Retreat:** Heated indoor and outdoor pools, saunas, and panoramic relaxation lounges.
- **Scenic Location:** Surrounded by picturesque hiking trails and dense Black Forest landscapes.

## 3. Burg Schwarzenstein (Rheingau – Near Heidelberg)

**Address:** Rosengasse 32, 65366 Geisenheim, Germany; **Check-in:** From 3:00 PM | **Check-out:** Until 12:00 PM; **Pricing:** Starting at €380 per night; **Dining:** Burgrestaurant (fine dining), Grill & Wine Bar (casual gourmet)

Why Stay Here?

For travelers seeking a castle experience with modern luxury, Burg Schwarzenstein offers an exceptional stay in a renovated medieval fortress with vineyard views.

**Key Features:**

- **Castle Atmosphere:** A mix of historic charm and contemporary elegance.
- **Exclusive Wine Experiences:** Located in one of Germany's top wine-growing regions.
- **Personalized Service:** A boutique hotel experience with tailored guest services.

## 4. Colombi Hotel (Freiburg im Breisgau)

**Address:** Rotteckring 16, 79098 Freiburg, Germany; **Check-in:** From 2:00 PM | **Check-out:** Until 12:00 PM; **Pricing:** Starting at €350 per night; **Dining:** Zirbelstube (Michelin-starred fine dining), Falkenstube (classic German dishes)

Why Stay Here?

Colombi Hotel is a blend of old-world charm and contemporary luxury in the heart of Freiburg, offering a refined experience for visitors exploring the city and the nearby Black Forest.

**Key Features:**

- **Prime Location:** Steps away from Freiburg's historic Old Town.
- **Michelin-Starred Cuisine:** Fine dining in the renowned Zirbelstube.
- **Wellness & Relaxation:** Indoor pool, sauna, and private wellness treatments.

## 5. Seehotel Überfahrt (Lake Constance – Bodensee)

**Address:** Überfahrtstraße 10, 83700 Rottach-Egern, Germany; **Check-in:** From 3:00 PM | **Check-out:** Until 11:00 AM; **Pricing:** Starting at €600 per night; **Dining:** Restaurant Überfahrt (Michelin-starred), Il Barcaiolo (Italian), Bayernstube (Bavarian specialties)

Why Stay Here?

Seehotel Überfahrt offers a five-star lakeside retreat on the shores of Lake Constance, combining alpine elegance with modern luxury.

**Key Features:**

- **Lakeside Luxury:** Stunning views and private access to the lake.
- **Gourmet Dining:** Home to multiple fine dining options, including Michelin-starred cuisine.
- **Spa & Wellness:** A 4,000 sqm wellness area with exclusive treatments.

## Mid-Range Hotels & Boutique Stays

### 1. Hotel Der Kleine Prinz (Baden-Baden)

**Address:** Lichtentaler Str. 36, 76530 Baden-Baden; **Check-in:** From 3:00 PM | **Check-out:** By 11:00 AM; **Price Range:** €150 – €220 per night; **Contact:** +49 7221 346600; **Website:** www.derkleineprinz.de

A romantic boutique hotel inspired by *The Little Prince*, this elegant stay offers a unique literary charm. Each room is individually decorated with classic furnishings, while modern amenities like free Wi-Fi, minibars, and room service enhance the experience. Located just a short walk from Lichtentaler Allee and the famous Baden-Baden thermal spas, this hotel provides easy access to the town's cultural and wellness attractions.

**Why Stay Here?**; ✔ Personalized service with a warm, intimate atmosphere; ✔ Excellent in-house restaurant offering gourmet cuisine; ✔ Prime location near Baden-Baden's top sights

## 2. Hotel Heiligenstein (Neuweier, Baden-Baden Wine Region)

📍 **Address:** Heiligensteinstr. 19a, 76534 Baden-Baden; 🕐 **Check-in:** From 3:00 PM | **Check-out:** By 11:00 AM; 💰 **Price Range:** €130 – €190 per night; 📞 **Contact:** +49 7223 80000; 🌐 **Website:** www.hotel-heiligenstein.de

Nestled in the picturesque vineyards of Neuweier, this boutique hotel is perfect for wine lovers. The cozy rooms are tastefully decorated, and some feature balconies overlooking the vineyards. The on-site spa, sauna, and restaurant serving regional specialties make it an excellent base for a relaxing getaway.

**Why Stay Here?**; ✔ Surrounded by stunning vineyards with excellent wine-tasting opportunities; ✔ In-house spa for relaxation; ✔ Great hiking and cycling routes nearby

## 3. Arthotel Heidelberg (Heidelberg)

📍 **Address:** Grabengasse 7, 69117 Heidelberg; 🕐 **Check-in:** From 2:00 PM | **Check-out:** By 12:00 PM; 💰 **Price Range:** €140 – €200 per night; 📞 **Contact:** +49 6221 650060; 🌐 **Website:** www.arthotel.de

A fusion of history and contemporary design, this stylish boutique hotel is set in a historic 18th-century building just minutes from Heidelberg Castle and the Old Bridge. The rooms feature a sleek, minimalist aesthetic with modern comforts, while the on-site *Romers Restaurant* serves fresh, regional cuisine.

**Why Stay Here?**; ✔ Walking distance to Heidelberg's most famous landmarks; ✔ Beautifully designed rooms with a mix of historic and modern elements; ✔ Rooftop terrace with city views

## 4. Hotel am Sophienpark (Baden-Baden)

📍 **Address:** Sophienstraße 14, 76530 Baden-Baden; 🕐 **Check-in:** From 3:00 PM | **Check-out:** By 11:00 AM; 💰 **Price Range:** €135 – €185 per night; 📞 **Contact:** +49 7221 3560; 🌐 **Website:** www.hotel-am-sophienpark.de

A refined hotel in a classic 19th-century building, Hotel am Sophienpark is an excellent mid-range choice in Baden-Baden. With spacious rooms, a private garden, and proximity to the Kurhaus Casino and Caracalla Spa, it offers a perfect balance of elegance and convenience.

**Why Stay Here?**; ✔ Prime location in Baden-Baden's center; ✔ Elegant garden terrace for breakfast and relaxation; ✔ Quiet yet close to major attractions

### 5. Hotel Hohenlohe (Schwäbisch Hall)

📍 **Address:** Weilertor 14, 74523 Schwäbisch Hall; 🕐 **Check-in:** From 3:00 PM | **Check-out:** By 11:00 AM; 💰 **Price Range:** €120 – €170 per night; 📞 **Contact:** +49 791 75870; 🌐 **Website:** www.hotel-hohenlohe.de

Overlooking the Kocher River, this charming boutique hotel offers spacious rooms, an excellent spa with thermal pools, and easy access to Schwäbisch Hall's medieval old town. The rooftop restaurant provides breathtaking views while serving local specialties.

**Why Stay Here?**; ✔ Spa with indoor and outdoor thermal pools; ✔ Stunning riverside views; ✔ Walkable distance to Schwäbisch Hall's historic sites

### 6. Domizil Tübingen (Tübingen)

📍 **Address:** Wöhrdstr. 5-9, 72072 Tübingen; 🕐 **Check-in:** From 3:00 PM | **Check-out:** By 11:00 AM; 💰 **Price Range:** €140 – €190 per night; 📞 **Contact:** +49 7071 13990; 🌐 **Website:** www.domizil-tuebingen.de

Set on the Neckar River, Domizil Tübingen is a stylish boutique hotel offering rooms with stunning views of the historic Altstadt. The interiors combine modern design with warm, welcoming touches, and the on-site bar is perfect for evening relaxation.

**Why Stay Here?**; ✔ Prime location with riverfront views; ✔ Walking distance to Tübingen's charming Old Town; ✔ Modern rooms with high-end amenities

## Budget Stays: Hostels & Guesthouses

### 1. DJH Youth Hostel Stuttgart International

🔑 **Address:** Haußmannstraße 27, 70188 Stuttgart; ☐ **Check-in:** 3:00 PM – 10:00 PM | **Check-out:** 7:00 AM – 10:00 AM; 💰 **Pricing:** From €35 per night (dormitory) | Private rooms from €65 per night; ☎ **Contact:** +49 711 6647470; 🌐 **Website:** jugendherberge.de

Located on a hill overlooking Stuttgart, this modern youth hostel is ideal for budget-conscious travelers who want easy access to the city while enjoying panoramic views. The hostel provides:

- **Amenities:** Free breakfast, luggage storage, lockers, free Wi-Fi, and a bar.
- **Room Options:** Mixed or female/male-only dormitories, as well as private rooms.
- **Nearby Attractions:** Schlossplatz (10-minute tram ride), Mercedes-Benz Museum (15 minutes), Stuttgart TV Tower (20 minutes).

### 2. Black Forest Hostel (Freiburg im Breisgau)

🔑 **Address:** Kartauserstraße 33, 79102 Freiburg; ☐ **Check-in:** 3:00 PM – 9:00 PM | **Check-out:** 7:30 AM – 11:00 AM; 💰 **Pricing:** Dorm beds from €22 per night | Private rooms from €55 per night; ☎ **Contact:** +49 761 881780; 🌐 **Website:** blackforest-hostel.de

For those exploring the Black Forest region, this budget hostel in Freiburg offers an affordable base with a relaxed atmosphere. Key features include:

- **Amenities:** Shared kitchen, communal lounge, outdoor terrace, laundry facilities, and bike rentals.
- **Room Options:** Large dorms (10–12 beds) and smaller private rooms.
- **Nearby Attractions:** Freiburg Minster (15-minute walk), Schlossberg (10-minute walk), Titisee Lake (40-minute train ride).

### 3. Hotel Bären (Meersburg, Lake Constance)

**Address:** Bismarckplatz 5, 88709 Meersburg; **Check-in:** 2:00 PM – 10:00 PM | **Check-out:** 7:30 AM – 11:00 AM; **Pricing:** Single rooms from €55 | Double rooms from €70; **Contact:** +49 7532 45040; **Website:** hotel-baeren-meersburg.de

A budget-friendly hotel near Lake Constance, Hotel Bären offers comfortable, no-frills lodging in one of the most scenic areas of Baden-Württemberg. Features include:

- **Amenities:** Free breakfast, Wi-Fi, luggage storage, and bike rental services.
- **Room Options:** Compact but well-furnished rooms with en-suite bathrooms.
- **Nearby Attractions:** Meersburg Castle (5-minute walk), Lake Constance promenade (3 minutes), Mainau Island (15-minute ferry ride).

### 4. Gästehaus Kaiserpassage (Karlsruhe)

**Address:** Kaiserpassage 10, 76133 Karlsruhe; **Check-in:** 3:00 PM – 9:00 PM | **Check-out:** 7:00 AM – 11:00 AM; **Pricing:** Dormitory beds from €30 | Private rooms from €55; ☎ **Contact:** +49 721 47001585; 🌐 **Website:** gaestehaus-kaiserpassage.de

This budget guesthouse is centrally located in Karlsruhe, making it a great choice for visitors exploring the city on a budget. Highlights include:

- **Amenities:** Shared kitchen, free Wi-Fi, common lounge area, and lockers.
- **Room Options:** Mixed dorms, female-only dorms, and simple private rooms.
- **Nearby Attractions:** Karlsruhe Palace (10-minute walk), ZKM Center for Art and Media (15 minutes), Durlach Old Town (20-minute tram ride).

**5. Hotel ibis Budget Mannheim Friedrichsfeld**

📍 **Address:** Langlachweg 18, 68229 Mannheim; **Check-in:** 3:00 PM – 10:00 PM | **Check-out:** 6:30 AM – 11:00 AM; 💰 **Pricing:** Double rooms from €55 per night; ☎ **Contact:** +49 621 483640; 🌐 **Website:** all.accor.com

This budget chain hotel is an excellent option for travelers needing an affordable yet comfortable stay near Mannheim. Key features include:

- **Amenities:** Free parking, Wi-Fi, air-conditioned rooms, and a breakfast buffet (€7 per person).
- **Room Options:** Compact double and twin rooms with private bathrooms.
- **Nearby Attractions:** Mannheim Palace (15-minute drive), Luisenpark (10 minutes), Technoseum (12 minutes).

**6. Pension Altstadtperle (Tübingen)**

📍 **Address:** Kornhausstraße 10, 72070 Tübingen; **Check-in:** 2:00 PM – 8:00 PM | **Check-out:** 8:00 AM – 11:00 AM; 💰 **Pricing:** Single rooms from €50 | Double rooms from €70; ☎ **Contact:** +49 7071 25201; ⊕ **Website:** altstadtperle-tuebingen.de

Located in the historic center of Tübingen, this cozy pension offers budget travelers a home-like stay with excellent accessibility. Key features include:

- **Amenities:** Free Wi-Fi, self-service kitchen, and luggage storage.
- **Room Options:** Individually decorated rooms with shared or private bathrooms.
- **Nearby Attractions:** Tübingen Castle (10-minute walk), Neckar River (5 minutes), Market Square (3 minutes).

## Unique Stays: Castles, Farm Stays & Spa Resorts

### 1. Burg Colmberg – A Night in a Medieval Castle

📍 **Address:** An der Burgenstraße, 91598 Colmberg, Germany; ⌂ **Check-in:** 3:00 PM | **Check-out:** 11:00 AM; 💰 **Price:** €140 – €350 per night (varies by season & room type); 🍽 **Dining:** On-site restaurant serving traditional Franconian cuisine

Perched atop a hill, **Burg Colmberg** offers an authentic medieval castle stay with thick stone walls, antique furnishings, and panoramic views of the surrounding countryside. Guests can sleep in rooms decorated with period-style furniture while enjoying modern comforts. The on-site restaurant specializes in wild game dishes, and the castle grounds invite exploration with historic courtyards and scenic walking trails. Ideal for history lovers and those seeking a fairytale-like experience.

## 2. Brenners Park-Hotel & Spa – A Royal Spa Retreat

📍 **Address:** Schillerstraße 4/6, 76530 Baden-Baden, Germany; 🏨 **Check-in:** 3:00 PM | **Check-out:** 12:00 PM; 💰 **Price:** €400 – €1,200 per night (luxury suite options available); 🍽 **Dining:** Michelin-starred dining at Wintergarten & Fritz & Felix

For those seeking ultimate relaxation, **Brenners Park-Hotel & Spa** in **Baden-Baden** is a world-class wellness retreat. This 5-star historic hotel, dating back to 1872, offers luxurious rooms with park views, access to the legendary spa town's thermal waters, and a full-service spa specializing in holistic treatments. The hotel's spa features an exclusive "Villa Stéphanie," a wellness sanctuary for detox, weight loss, and relaxation therapies. The in-house restaurant, **Fritz & Felix**, delivers gourmet cuisine with locally sourced ingredients.

## 3. Hotel Traube Tonbach – Traditional Black Forest Elegance

📍 **Address:** Tonbachstraße 237, 72270 Baiersbronn, Germany; 🏨 **Check-in:** 2:00 PM | **Check-out:** 11:00 AM; 💰 **Price:** €250 – €800 per night (includes breakfast & spa access); 🍽 **Dining:** Home to the 3-Michelin-starred restaurant, Schwarzwaldstube

Located in the heart of the **Black Forest**, **Hotel Traube Tonbach** is a family-run luxury retreat with over 230 years of tradition. The property features spacious rooms with scenic balcony views, a renowned wellness area with multiple saunas, and direct access to hiking trails. Its biggest highlight is the **Schwarzwaldstube**, one of Germany's most prestigious Michelin-starred restaurants, offering an unforgettable fine dining experience.

## 4. Weingut Hotel Restaurant Schlossberg – A Stay Among Vineyards

📍 **Address:** Schlossbergstraße 3, 79235 Vogtsburg, Germany; 🏨 **Check-in:** 3:00 PM | **Check-out:** 11:00 AM; 💰 **Price:** €120 – €250 per night (includes breakfast & wine tasting); 🍽 **Dining:** On-site winery restaurant with regional specialties

Nestled in **Kaiserstuhl's wine country**, this boutique hotel allows guests to stay amidst vineyards while enjoying direct access to local winemakers. Each room features rustic yet modern décor with vineyard views. The hotel offers guided wine tastings, seasonal grape harvest experiences, and exclusive wine pairing dinners. Ideal for wine enthusiasts and couples looking for a romantic getaway.

### 5. Altes Pfarrhaus – A Converted Historic Parsonage

📍 **Address:** Kirchstraße 1, 75015 Bretten, Germany; 🏨 **Check-in:** 4:00 PM | **Check-out:** 10:30 AM; 💰 **Price:** €100 – €180 per night (special discounts for extended stays); 🍽 **Dining:** Complimentary breakfast with fresh local produce

For travelers seeking a **boutique historical stay**, **Altes Pfarrhaus** is a beautifully restored **17th-century parsonage** that retains its timber-frame charm while offering modern comforts. Located in a picturesque village, this intimate guesthouse features cozy fireplaces, wooden beams, and a tranquil garden. The owners provide personalized service, making it an excellent choice for cultural travelers looking for an off-the-beaten-path retreat.

### 6. V8 Hotel – A Car Lover's Dream

📍 **Address:** Graf-Zeppelin-Platz 1, 71034 Böblingen, Germany; 🏨 **Check-in:** 3:00 PM | **Check-out:** 12:00 PM; 💰 **Price:** €160 – €450 per night (themed suites available); 🍽 **Dining:** On-site restaurant with German & international cuisine

Located within Stuttgart's **Motorworld Region**, this **automobile-themed hotel** is perfect for car enthusiasts. Each room is decorated with automotive elements, from classic car-shaped beds to garages showcasing rare vintage vehicles. The hotel is just a short drive from the **Mercedes-Benz and Porsche Museums**, making it an ideal stay for auto lovers visiting Baden-Württemberg.

## 7. Mühle zu Gersbach – A Secluded Millhouse Stay

**Address:** Gersbachstraße 60, 79650 Schopfheim, Germany; **Check-in:** 3:00 PM | **Check-out:** 11:00 AM; **Price:** €130 – €300 per night (includes breakfast & hiking tours); **Dining:** Traditional Black Forest cuisine with fresh ingredients

For a **peaceful countryside escape**, **Mühle zu Gersbach** offers a stay in a converted **historic watermill** surrounded by forests, meadows, and hiking trails. The guesthouse provides **guided nature walks**, authentic **Swabian meals**, and a warm, rustic atmosphere. It's an excellent choice for those looking to disconnect from city life and experience the serenity of the Black Forest.

## 8. Baumhaushotel Schwarzwald – A Treehouse Escape

**Address:** Tannenweg 1, 72250 Freudenstadt, Germany; **Check-in:** 3:00 PM | **Check-out:** 11:00 AM; **Price:** €180 – €350 per night (includes breakfast & adventure activities); **Dining:** Self-catering facilities & local restaurant partnerships

For a **nature-immersed experience**, the **Baumhaushotel Schwarzwald** offers eco-friendly **treehouse lodges** deep in the **Black Forest**. These elevated wooden cabins provide **360° forest views**, cozy interiors, and easy access to outdoor activities like zip-lining, hiking, and wildlife spotting. Perfect for adventurous travelers and families.

# CHAPTER 5.

# RESTAURANTS, FOOD & DINING, MUST-TASTE CUISINES

## Must-Taste Cuisines:

**1. Maultaschen (Swabian Dumplings)**

A specialty of Swabia, Maultaschen are large ravioli-like pasta pockets filled with a mix of minced meat, spinach, bread crumbs, and herbs. Traditionally served in broth or pan-fried with onions and butter, this dish is sometimes referred to as the "Swabian answer to Italian ravioli."

📍 **Where to Try It:**

- **Gasthaus Zur Linde** (Schwäbisch Hall); 📍 Address: Obere Herrngasse 6, 74523 Schwäbisch Hall; ☐ Opening Hours: 11:30 AM – 10:00 PM (Closed on Mondays); 💰 Price Range: €12 – €18
- **Weinstube Kachelofen** (Stuttgart); 📍 Address: Eberhardstraße 10, 70173 Stuttgart; ☐ Opening Hours: 12:00 PM – 11:00 PM; 💰 Price Range: €14 – €20

## 2. Spätzle (Egg Noodles)

A staple of Swabian cuisine, Spätzle are soft, chewy egg noodles that are often served as a side dish with meat or in their popular cheesy version, Käsespätzle. The best Spätzle are handmade and have a rich, buttery texture.

📍 **Where to Try It:**

- **Gasthof Zum Hirsch** (Tübingen); 📍 Address: Marktgasse 4, 72070 Tübingen; ☐ Opening Hours: 12:00 PM – 10:30 PM; 💰 Price Range: €9 – €16
- **S'Kicherle** (Ulm); 📍 Address: Hafengasse 19, 89073 Ulm; ☐ Opening Hours: 11:30 AM – 10:00 PM; 💰 Price Range: €11 – €17

## 3. Schwarzwälder Kirschtorte (Black Forest Cake)

This iconic dessert originates from the Black Forest region and is made with layers of chocolate sponge cake, whipped cream, and cherries, infused with the region's famous Kirschwasser (cherry brandy).

📍 **Where to Try It:**

- **Café Schäfer** (Triberg) – Home to the Original Recipe; 📍 Address: Hauptstraße 33, 78098 Triberg; ☐ Opening Hours: 10:00 AM – 6:00 PM; 💰 Price Range: €5 – €8 per slice
- **Café König** (Baden-Baden); 📍 Address: Lichtentaler Str. 12, 76530 Baden-Baden; ☐ Opening Hours: 9:00 AM – 7:00 PM; 💰 Price Range: €4.50 – €7 per slice

## 4. Zwiebelrostbraten (Onion Roast Beef)

A hearty dish of pan-seared beef topped with crispy fried onions, served with Spätzle and a rich, flavorful gravy. This dish is deeply rooted in Swabian culinary traditions and is a must-try for meat lovers.

📍 **Where to Try It:**

- **Alte Kanzlei** (Stuttgart); 📍 Address: Schillerplatz 5, 70173 Stuttgart; 🕐 Opening Hours: 11:30 AM – 11:00 PM; 💰 Price Range: €22 – €30
- **Restaurant Ratskeller** (Freiburg); 📍 Address: Münsterplatz 6, 79098 Freiburg; 🕐 Opening Hours: 12:00 PM – 10:30 PM; 💰 Price Range: €19 – €28

## 5. Käsespätzle (Cheese Noodles)

A rich, creamy dish where Spätzle is layered with melted cheese (often Emmental) and topped with crispy fried onions. It's the Swabian version of macaroni and cheese, but far more indulgent.

📍 **Where to Try It:**

- **Restaurant Gerberhaus** (Rottweil); 📍 Address: Hauptstraße 18, 78628 Rottweil; 🕐 Opening Hours: 11:00 AM – 9:00 PM; 💰 Price Range: €12 – €18
- **Wirtshaus zur Brezel** (Karlsruhe); 📍 Address: Kaiserstraße 220, 76133 Karlsruhe; 🕐 Opening Hours: 12:00 PM – 10:00 PM; 💰 Price Range: €11 – €16

## 6. Flammkuchen (Alsatian-Style Pizza)

Although originating from the Alsace region, Flammkuchen is incredibly popular in Baden-Württemberg. This thin, crispy flatbread is traditionally topped with crème fraîche, onions, and bacon.

📍 **Where to Try It:**

- **Flammerie** (Heidelberg); 📍 Address: Hauptstraße 192, 69117 Heidelberg; 🕐 Opening Hours: 12.00 PM – 10:30 PM; 💰 Price Range: €10 – €15
- **Zur Sonne** (Freiburg); 📍 Address: Gerberau 46, 79098 Freiburg; 🕐 Opening Hours: 5:00 PM – 11:00 PM; 💰 Price Range: €9 – €14

### 7. Schupfnudeln (Potato Dumplings)

These thick, hand-rolled potato dumplings are typically pan-fried with sauerkraut and bacon, creating a crispy, golden texture with a balance of smoky and sour flavors.

📍 **Where to Try It:**

- **Zum Seppl** (Heidelberg); 📍 Address: Hauptstraße 213, 69117 Heidelberg; ☐ Opening Hours: 11:00 AM – 11:00 PM; 💰 Price Range: €12 – €18
- **Gasthaus Löwen** (Baden-Baden); 📍 Address: Lichtentaler Str. 94, 76530 Baden-Baden; ☐ Opening Hours: 12:00 PM – 10:00 PM; 💰 Price Range: €11 – €17

## Best Restaurants in Baden-Württemberg

### 1. Schwarzwaldstube (3 Michelin Stars) – Baiersbronn

📍 **Address:** Tonbachstraße 237, 72270 Baiersbronn; ⏰ **Opening Hours:** Wednesday – Sunday: 12:00 PM – 2:00 PM, 7:00 PM – 10:00 PM | Closed Monday & Tuesday; 💰 **Pricing:** €250+ per person for the tasting menu; 🍽 **Specialties:** Seasonal tasting menu featuring Black Forest trout, venison, and luxurious foie gras

Schwarzwaldstube, the crown jewel of Baiersbronn's renowned culinary scene, offers **haute cuisine with a regional twist**. This **three-Michelin-starred** restaurant is famous for its elegant interpretation of Swabian flavors, using premium local ingredients. The restaurant's philosophy is rooted in precision, refinement, and an emphasis on **seasonal produce from the Black Forest region**. Expect dishes like

**Black Forest venison with lingonberry sauce** or **butter-soft Atlantic turbot with saffron foam**.

## 2. Restaurant Ophelia (2 Michelin Stars) – Konstanz

📍 **Address:** Inselstraße 12, 78462 Konstanz; 🕐 **Opening Hours:** Wednesday – Saturday: 6:00 PM – 10:00 PM | Closed Sunday – Tuesday; 💰 **Pricing:** €160 – €220 per person; 🍽 **Specialties:** Fine seafood dishes, caviar, and gourmet vegetarian plates

Located in a historic Art Nouveau villa overlooking **Lake Constance**, Restaurant Ophelia blends **sophistication with lakeside charm**. Chef Dirk Hoberg curates an exquisite multi-course menu that often includes **Lake Constance char with fennel pollen** and **hand-dived scallops with a citrus beurre blanc. The wine pairings are exceptional**, featuring **Rieslings from the Baden vineyards**.

## 3. Gasthaus zur Linde (Traditional Swabian Cuisine) – Stuttgart

📍 **Address:** Gablenberger Hauptstraße 109, 70186 Stuttgart; 🕐 **Opening Hours:** Monday – Saturday: 11:30 AM – 10:30 PM | Sunday: 12:00 PM – 9:00 PM; 💰 **Pricing:** €20 – €45 per person; 🍽 **Specialties:** Maultaschen, Käsespätzle, Zwiebelrostbraten

For **authentic Swabian comfort food**, Gasthaus zur Linde is a **must-visit**. This **century-old tavern** is known for **handmade Maultaschen (Swabian dumplings)**, served either pan-fried with onions or in a rich broth. The **Zwiebelrostbraten (onion roast beef)** is a local favorite, cooked to perfection and served with crispy fried onions and buttery spätzle. **Rustic wooden interiors and friendly service** make this a cozy spot for travelers craving traditional flavors.

## 4. Restaurant Bareiss (3 Michelin Stars) – Baiersbronn

📍 **Address:** Hermine-Bareiss-Weg 1, 72270 Baiersbronn; 🕐 **Opening Hours:** Wednesday – Sunday: 6:00 PM – 10:00 PM | Closed Monday &

Tuesday; 💰 **Pricing:** €280+ per person; 🍽 **Specialties:** Gourmet Swabian-French fusion cuisine

Another **culinary legend** in Baiersbronn, Bareiss combines **classic French techniques with regional ingredients**. Signature dishes include **Black Forest venison carpaccio**, **lobster ravioli in saffron sauce**, and **milk-fed lamb from the Swabian Alb**. The ambiance is **sophisticated yet inviting**, with attentive service and an **extensive wine selection** featuring both local and international vintages.

**5. Schlossberg Restaurant (1 Michelin Star) – Baiersbronn**

📍 **Address:** Murgtalstraße 602, 72270 Baiersbronn; 🕐 **Opening Hours:** Thursday – Monday: 6:30 PM – 10:00 PM | Closed Tuesday & Wednesday; 💰 **Pricing:** €140 – €180 per person; 🍽 **Specialties:** Seasonal tasting menu, locally sourced game, and artisanal cheese pairings

Nestled in the Black Forest, Schlossberg Restaurant is **renowned for its elegant yet approachable fine dining**. The **chef emphasizes seasonal and organic ingredients**, crafting dishes such as **wild Black Forest mushrooms with truffle-infused risotto** and **roasted saddle of venison with elderberry jus**. The **cheese cart is a highlight**, featuring hand-selected **Baden-Württemberg dairy specialties**.

**6. Weinstube Fröhlich (Authentic Wine Tavern) – Heidelberg**

📍 **Address:** Hauptstraße 134, 69117 Heidelberg; 🕐 **Opening Hours:** Monday – Sunday: 5:00 PM – 11:00 PM; 💰 **Pricing:** €15 – €35 per person; 🍽 **Specialties:** Hearty German platters, schnitzels, and regional wines

A **charming, family-run weinstube (wine tavern)** in the heart of **Heidelberg's Old Town**, Weinstube Fröhlich is the perfect place for **casual, traditional dining**. Their **Wiener Schnitzel** is pan-fried to a crisp golden brown, served with potato salad and lingonberry compote. **The extensive wine list** features local varietals like

**Trollinger, Riesling, and Lemberger**, sourced directly from **Baden-Württemberg's vineyards**.

## 7. Esszimmer (Contemporary Fine Dining) – Karlsruhe

📍 **Address:** Bahnhofstraße 14, 76137 Karlsruhe; 🕐 **Opening Hours:** Tuesday – Saturday: 6:00 PM – 11:00 PM | Closed Sunday & Monday; 💰 **Pricing:** €90 – €150 per person; 🍽 **Specialties:** Seasonal tasting menu with modern German influences

For an **innovative take on German cuisine**, Esszimmer in Karlsruhe is a **standout choice**. The **menu changes seasonally**, but past highlights include **beetroot-cured salmon with horseradish foam**, **dry-aged duck breast with cranberry glaze**, and **sous-vide pork belly with apple cider reduction**. **Minimalist yet stylish interiors**, impeccable service, and carefully curated wine pairings make for a **memorable dining experience**.

# CHAPTER 6.

# MUST-SEE ATTRACTIONS & HIDDEN GEMS

**1. Heidelberg Castle**

**Address:** Schlossweg 1, 69117 Heidelberg; **Opening Hours:** Daily 8:00 AM – 6:00 PM (April – October), 10:00 AM – 5:00 PM (November – March); **Pricing:** Adults €9, Reduced €4.50, Family Ticket €20; **Dining Options:** Schlossrestaurant for local cuisine with panoramic views; **Accommodation:** Several nearby hotels such as Hotel Ritter and Hotel Zum Ritter St. Georg

Heidelberg Castle, perched above the Neckar River, is an iconic symbol of the region. A fascinating blend of Gothic and Renaissance architecture, this castle offers a breathtaking view over the city of Heidelberg. It's renowned for its imposing structure, the impressive German Pharmacy Museum, and the beautiful castle gardens. Visitors can explore the castle's tower, the large courtyard, and the Great Barrel, the world's largest wine barrel. The castle is accessible by foot or the funicular railway.

**2. Black Forest (Schwarzwald)**

**Address:** The Black Forest region spans from Freiburg to Pforzheim; **Opening Hours:** Open year-round, depending on weather conditions; **Pricing:** Free entry, though some attractions (such as the Triberg Waterfalls) may charge entry fees; **Dining Options:** Traditional eateries like Gasthof zum Jäger in Triberg; **Accommodation:** Black Forest resorts, boutique hotels, and cozy cabins

The Black Forest is not just a forest, but an expansive area of rolling hills, dense woods, and picturesque villages. It offers a range of outdoor activities such as hiking, cycling, and skiing in the winter months. The scenic Schwarzwaldhochstraße (High Road) provides some of the best views in the region. Key highlights include the Triberg Waterfalls, the quaint town of Baden-Baden with its spas, and the charming village of Gengenbach, famous for its medieval architecture.

### 3. Lake Constance (Bodensee)

**Address:** The lake spans the borders of Germany, Austria, and Switzerland, with access from towns like Konstanz and Friedrichshafen; **Opening Hours:** Open year-round, with boat tours running April – October; **Pricing:** Boat tours starting from €20; **Dining Options:** Lakeside restaurants such as Restaurant Seeblick in Konstanz; **Accommodation:** Lakeside hotels, including Steigenberger Inselhotel in Konstanz

Lake Constance is one of Europe's largest lakes, offering stunning views and a range of recreational activities. Visitors can take boat tours to explore the picturesque towns around the lake, visit the famous Mainau Island with its gardens and butterfly house, or take a bike ride along the lake's many cycling paths. The region is also home to vineyards and is known for its fish-based cuisine, such as Bodensee perch.

### 4. Stuttgart's Mercedes-Benz & Porsche Museums

**Address:**

- Mercedes-Benz Museum: Mercedesstraße 100, 70372 Stuttgart
- Porsche Museum: Porscheplatz 1, 70435 Stuttgart; **Opening Hours:** Mercedes-Benz Museum: Daily 9:00 AM – 6:00 PM,

Porsche Museum: Tuesday – Sunday 9:00 AM – 6:00 PM; **Pricing:**

- Mercedes-Benz Museum: Adults €10, Reduced €4
- Porsche Museum: Adults €10, Reduced €4; **Dining Options:** Café in Mercedes-Benz Museum and Porsche Museum; **Accommodation:** Design hotel such as Jaz in the City

These two automotive museums offer an extraordinary look at the history of two iconic brands. The Mercedes-Benz Museum, spanning from the car's inception in the 1880s to the present, showcases over 160 vehicles, while the Porsche Museum focuses on the legendary cars and their role in motorsport history. Both museums offer an immersive experience into the world of automotive engineering and design, with interactive exhibits and historical artifacts.

## 5. Hohenzollern Castle

**Address:** Burg Hohenzollern, 72379 Burg Hohenzollern; **Opening Hours:** Daily 9:00 AM – 6:00 PM (March – October), 10:00 AM – 4:00 PM (November – February); **Pricing:** Adults €13, Children €4; **Dining Options:** Castle café with regional specialties; **Accommodation:** Nearby hotels in the Swabian Alps

Perched atop Mount Hohenzollern, this fairy-tale castle is one of the most picturesque in Germany. With its towers and spires, it offers not just incredible history but also one of the most panoramic views in Baden-Württemberg. Inside, visitors can admire the magnificent rooms, royal artifacts, and splendid artwork, while also exploring the surrounding nature trails. The castle also hosts annual medieval festivals that immerse visitors in historical reenactments.

## 6. Freiburg's Historic Old Town

**Address:** Freiburg im Breisgau, 79098 Freiburg; **Opening Hours:** Open year-round; **Pricing:** Free to explore the Old Town; **Dining Options:** Try local specialties at the Gasthof Zum Kranz or traditional taverns along the streets; **Accommodation:** Stay at the Hotel Oberkirch with views of the cathedral

Freiburg's Old Town is a delightful maze of cobbled streets, colorful buildings, and centuries-old houses. At the heart of the Old Town lies the magnificent Freiburg Minster, a Gothic cathedral with stunning stained-glass windows and a towering spire. The surrounding area is dotted with local shops, cafes, and the famous "Bächle" – small water channels running along the streets. It's an excellent place to soak in the atmosphere and enjoy local food, including the regional specialty, Flammkuchen (a type of thin-crust pizza).

### 7. Ulm Minster

**Address:** Münsterplatz 1, 89073 Ulm; **Opening Hours:** Daily 9:00 AM – 5:00 PM (April – October), 10:00 AM – 4:00 PM (November – March); **Pricing:** Free entry, but a small fee is required to climb the tower; **Dining Options:** Local restaurants like Gasthof Rössle; **Accommodation:** Stay in Ulm's historic center, such as at the Maritim Hotel

The Ulm Minster, famous for having the tallest church steeple in the world, dominates the skyline of Ulm. Visitors can climb the 768 steps to the top of the tower for panoramic views of the city and beyond. The interior is equally impressive, with beautiful stained-glass windows and intricate architecture. Its location next to the Danube River makes it perfect for exploring the surrounding areas, including the picturesque Fishermen's Quarter.

## Hidden Gems:

### 1. Wiblingen Abbey Library

- **Address:** Wiblingen Abbey, Ulm, Baden-Württemberg
- **Opening Times:** Daily, 10:00 AM - 5:00 PM

- **Price:** Adults: €6, Reduced: €3, Children (under 12): Free
- **Description:** Tucked away in the charming town of Ulm, Wiblingen Abbey's library is a Baroque masterpiece that remains relatively under the radar. The stunning Rococo library, adorned with ornate frescoes and intricate woodwork, is a prime example of 18th-century religious art. The Abbey itself was once a Benedictine monastery, and its library holds rare medieval manuscripts.
- **Why Visit?** Its secluded location and the preserved beauty of its interiors make it one of the most impressive examples of Baroque architecture in the region.

## 2. Maulbronn Monastery

- **Address:** Maulbronn, 75433 Baden-Württemberg
- **Opening Times:** April - October: 9:00 AM - 6:00 PM, November - March: 10:00 AM - 5:00 PM
- **Price:** Adults: €10, Reduced: €8, Children: €3
- **Description:** A UNESCO World Heritage site, Maulbronn Monastery is an architectural jewel of the Middle Ages. This former Cistercian monastery, founded in the 12th century, is one of the best-preserved of its kind in Europe. Wander through the well-maintained cloisters, abbey church, and ancient halls. The tranquility of the site, combined with the medieval surroundings, provides an almost mystical experience.
- **Why Visit?** The monastery offers not only a step back in time but also some of the most peaceful and reflective moments in the region.

## 3. Esslingen's Medieval Wine Cellars

- **Address:** Esslingen am Neckar, 73728 Baden-Württemberg

- **Opening Times:** Monday - Saturday: 10:00 AM - 6:00 PM
- **Price:** Guided Tours: €10, Tasting Experience: €15
- **Description:** Nestled beneath the town of Esslingen, these medieval wine cellars are an underrated gem. The cellar tours allow visitors to explore hundreds of years of winemaking history. Esslingen is part of the Württemberg wine region, known for its fine reds, especially the Lemberger variety. During the tour, you can sample wines directly from the source and learn about the centuries-old traditions of winemaking in this area.
- **Why Visit?** The unique combination of history and local wine culture makes this experience stand out, especially for wine enthusiasts.

4. Lichtenstein Castle

- **Address:** Lichtenstein Castle, 72805 Württemberg
- **Opening Times:** April - October: 9:00 AM - 6:00 PM, November - March: 10:00 AM - 4:00 PM
- **Price:** Adults: €12, Reduced: €7, Children: €5
- **Description:** Often referred to as the "Fairy Tale Castle," Lichtenstein Castle is perched dramatically on a cliff in the Swabian Alps. The romantic medieval architecture of this castle, with its high towers and narrow passageways, looks like it's straight out of a storybook. Its design was inspired by the novel "Lichtenstein" by Wilhelm Hauff, giving it a truly ethereal quality.
- **Why Visit?** The breathtaking views of the surrounding countryside and the castle's picturesque beauty make it a photographer's dream and a great escape from the crowds.

## 5. Triberg Waterfalls

- **Address:** Triberg, 78098 Baden-Württemberg
- **Opening Times:** Open daily from 9:00 AM to 7:00 PM
- **Price:** €3 per adult, Free for children under 6
- **Description:** Hidden deep within the Black Forest, Triberg Waterfalls are some of Germany's highest, with a drop of over 160 meters. The trails leading to the falls offer a unique opportunity to witness the beauty of the forest while listening to the sound of rushing water. The falls themselves are surrounded by lush greenery, making it an ideal destination for nature lovers and photographers.
- **Why Visit?** If you're looking for an immersive experience in nature, the Triberg Waterfalls offer a tranquil escape, away from the usual tourist sites. Don't forget to visit the nearby Black Forest Museum for more insight into the region's culture and natural history.

## 6. Schwetzingen Palace & Gardens

- **Address:** Schwetzingen Palace, 68723 Baden-Württemberg
- **Opening Times:** April - October: 9:00 AM - 6:00 PM, November - March: 10:00 AM - 4:00 PM
- **Price:** Adults: €8, Children (under 18): Free
- **Description:** Located near Heidelberg, Schwetzingen Palace is renowned for its exquisite gardens, which are considered some of the finest in Germany. The palace itself is an 18th-century Baroque building, but it's the formal gardens that truly capture the essence of this hidden gem. With perfectly manicured lawns, romantic pavilions, and an impressive collection of sculptures, this site is perfect for those who appreciate art and nature.

- **Why Visit?** The combination of history, architecture, and beautifully landscaped gardens makes it an ideal spot for relaxation and exploration.

**7. The Caves of the Swabian Jura (Swabian Alps)**
- **Address:** Swabian Jura, Baden-Württemberg
- **Opening Times:** Varies by site
- **Price:** Entry: Varies by location (€3–€6)
- **Description:** The caves of the Swabian Jura, a UNESCO World Heritage site, are home to some of the world's oldest known human-made artifacts. These caves, like the famous Hohle Fels and Vogelherd, have yielded artifacts from prehistoric times, including the earliest known sculptures of human figures. Visitors can explore the natural beauty of these limestone caves and learn about their significance in human history.
- **Why Visit?** For history buffs and those fascinated by prehistoric cultures, this hidden gem offers a unique opportunity to explore the birthplace of modern humanity.

# CHAPTER 7.

# Cultural Activities & Experiences

## Traditional Swabian Festivals & Events

**1. Stuttgart Beer Festival (Stuttgarter Frühlingsfest)**
- **Location:** Wasen, Stuttgart
- **Opening Times:** April – May (usually around 3 weeks)
- **Pricing:** Free entry, with costs for food, drinks, and rides
- **Details:** Often referred to as "the little Oktoberfest," Stuttgart Beer Festival is a lively, family-friendly event that takes place every spring in the heart of the Swabian capital. Visitors can enjoy a variety of German beers, local food such as bratwurst and pretzels, and a lively carnival atmosphere complete with rides and traditional folk music. The festival showcases a broad array of local and international brews, along with Swabian delicacies that cater to all tastes.

## 2. Swabian Fasnet (Carnival)

- **Location:** Primarily in the Swabian-Alb region, including cities like Rottweil and Überlingen
- **Opening Times:** January – February, with key dates around the week leading up to Ash Wednesday
- **Pricing:** Free to attend most events; some areas may charge for special performances or seating
- **Details:** Swabian Fasnet is the Swabian region's interpretation of Carnival, one of the oldest and most significant festivals in Baden-Württemberg. Originating in medieval traditions, it features elaborate costumes, parades, traditional masked dances, and music. The Rottweiler Fasnet parade is particularly famous, with its unique masks made of wood and the local "Zunft" or guilds playing central roles. Traditional figures like the "Narr" (fool) are seen throughout the region, embodying the spirit of rebellion and festivity before Lent.

## 3. Stuttgart Wine Festival (Stuttgarter Weindorf)

- **Location:** Schlossplatz, Stuttgart
- **Opening Times:** August – September (typically 10 days)
- **Pricing:** Free entry, but charges apply for wine tasting and food
- **Details:** For those with a love for wine, the Stuttgart Wine Festival is an unmissable event. Held annually in the city's Schlossplatz square, it celebrates the region's wine culture, particularly the vineyards that dot the surrounding hills. Visitors can sample a wide selection of Swabian wines, enjoy live music, and indulge in local specialties like "Maultaschen" and "Kässpätzle." The festival is a perfect opportunity to immerse in the Swabian tradition of wine-making, with local producers offering exclusive tastings of their most prized vintages.

**4. Ulm Festival (Ulm Festival of Music and Theatre)**
- **Location:** Various locations in Ulm, including the Ulm Theatre and city squares
- **Opening Times:** June – August (Summer months)
- **Pricing:** Varies by performance; tickets range from €15–€50
- **Details:** Ulm's Festival of Music and Theatre offers an outstanding celebration of local culture and artistic expression. It includes a series of performances, including opera, symphonies, and traditional Swabian folk music. Performances often take place in the historic settings of Ulm, such as the Ulm Theatre and around the famed Ulm Minster. This festival is an opportunity for visitors to engage with Swabian art and culture in one of the region's most scenic cities, with performances that blend classical with contemporary Swabian influences.

**5. Heilbronn Garlic Market (Knoblauchmarkt)**
- **Location:** Heilbronn City Centre
- **Opening Times:** May (usually one weekend)
- **Pricing:** Free entry, with costs for food and local products
- **Details:** Unique to the Heilbronn region, this market is a homage to garlic, a key ingredient in many Swabian dishes. It's a fun, quirky festival where visitors can sample everything from garlic-infused sausages to garlic bread and pickled garlic. Visitors can also purchase local crafts and artisan products, many of which incorporate garlic. The market also features live music, folk dancing, and cooking demonstrations focused on local culinary traditions.

**6. Ludwigsburg Pumpkin Festival (Ludwigsburger Kürbisausstellung)**
- **Location:** Blühendes Barock, Ludwigsburg
- **Opening Times:** September – November

- **Pricing:** Adult tickets €14, children €8
- **Details:** The Ludwigsburg Pumpkin Festival is one of the world's largest of its kind, showcasing over 500 varieties of pumpkins. Set in the beautiful Baroque gardens of Ludwigsburg Palace, the event is a feast for the eyes, with elaborate pumpkin sculptures and decorative displays throughout the grounds. Beyond just pumpkin displays, the festival also offers workshops, pumpkin carving contests, and seasonal foods such as pumpkin soup and pumpkin pie.

## 7. Schwäbischer Albverein (Swabian Jura Association Events)

- **Location:** Various towns across the Swabian Jura, such as Albstadt, Reutlingen, and Tübingen
- **Opening Times:** Year-round, with specific hiking tours and festivals held throughout the seasons
- **Pricing:** Often free or minimal fees for guided tours and events
- **Details:** For outdoor enthusiasts, the Schwäbischer Albverein offers year-round activities that highlight the natural beauty and traditions of the Swabian Jura mountain range. This includes guided hiking tours, local folklore festivals, and cultural events celebrating the region's history and folklore. The association also organizes community feasts and markets that promote local produce, crafts, and Swabian traditions.

## 8. Tübingen Medieval Market (Mittelaltermarkt)

- **Location:** Tübingen City Centre
- **Opening Times:** September
- **Pricing:** Free entry
- **Details:** Tübingen's Medieval Market transports visitors back to the Middle Ages, showcasing the city's medieval roots through reenactments, craft demonstrations, and medieval

music. Vendors dress in period costumes and sell traditional goods, from hand-forged swords to herbal remedies and medieval attire. The market also features live jousting and performances of medieval plays. This festival is perfect for history buffs or anyone who wants to experience the medieval atmosphere that once defined many towns in Baden-Württemberg.

# Wine Tasting in the Vineyards of Baden

Key Locations for Wine Tasting in Baden

### 1. Weingut Dr. Heger – Kappelrodeck

- **Address**: Kappelrodeck, Baden-Württemberg, 77876, Germany
- **Opening Times**: Monday to Saturday, 10:00 AM to 6:00 PM; Closed on Sundays.
- **Pricing**: €15 - €30 for a guided wine tasting session. Special rates for group bookings.
- **Contact**: +49 7842 9980
- **Website**: www.weingut-heger.de

At Weingut Dr. Heger, visitors can enjoy an intimate tour of the vineyard, learning about sustainable practices in winemaking while sampling some of the best local wines. The estate is known for its high-quality Pinot Noir and Riesling, with tastings offered either outdoors in the scenic vineyard or inside the wine cellar.

### 2. Weingut Schloss Neuweier – Baden-Baden

- **Address**: Schloss Neuweier, Baden-Baden, 76534, Germany

- **Opening Times**: Tuesday to Saturday, 10:00 AM to 5:00 PM; Closed on Sundays and Mondays.
- **Pricing**: €18 - €45 per person for guided tours and tastings.
- **Contact**: +49 7221 967760
- **Website**: www.weingut-schloss-neuweier.de

Set against the backdrop of the historic Neuweier Castle, this vineyard combines history and fine wine. With its rich tradition of winemaking, guests can enjoy wine tastings in the castle's wine cellar, with a selection of red and white wines. The highlight here is their excellent Pinot Noir and Baden Sauvignon Blanc.

### 3. Weingut Franz Keller – Oberbergen

- **Address**: Oberbergen, Baden-Württemberg, 79235, Germany
- **Opening Times**: Monday to Friday, 9:00 AM to 6:00 PM; Saturday, 10:00 AM to 4:00 PM.
- **Pricing**: €20 - €35 for tastings and tours.
- **Contact**: +49 7642 91010
- **Website**: www.franzkeller.de

This winery, established in 1789, offers a hands-on winemaking experience with its guided tours. Guests can explore both the vineyards and the winery's cellars, where they can taste a range of Baden wines. This vineyard is particularly known for its high-quality Spätburgunder (Pinot Noir) and Chardonnays.

Wine Tasting Experience in Baden

Wine tasting in Baden is about more than just drinking wine; it's an immersive cultural experience that offers insight into the region's history, terroir, and passion for winemaking. Here's a deeper dive into what you can expect during a wine tasting visit:

**Guided Vineyard Tours**

Most wineries in Baden offer guided tours where guests can explore the rolling vineyards with expert guides. The guides provide an in-depth understanding of the region's unique terroir, the history of the wine estates, and the winemaking process. Many of the vineyards are perched on the steep slopes of the Black Forest, giving visitors panoramic views of the countryside as they walk among the vines.

**Wine Tasting Sessions**

Tastings are typically organized in a charming cellar or an outdoor patio overlooking the vineyards. Wine enthusiasts are led through a curated selection of wines, from dry whites like Müller-Thurgau to rich, earthy reds like Pinot Noir. The tasting session often includes an educational explanation of each wine's characteristics, how it was made, and how it pairs with local cuisine.

**Must-Taste Wines**

1. **Pinot Noir (Spätburgunder)**: Baden's flagship red wine, characterized by its delicate aroma, fine tannins, and deep ruby color. It is one of the best places in Germany to taste Spätburgunder, especially around the Kaiserstuhl region.

2. **Riesling**: The region's cool climate lends itself well to Riesling, producing wines that are aromatic, refreshing, and often with a touch of sweetness.

3. **Chardonnay**: Baden's warm climate allows for the production of some exceptional Chardonnays, often with complex, oaky notes and rich textures.

4. **Trollinger**: A unique red wine from Baden, known for its light, fruity character and is a favorite for casual drinking.

### Wine Pairing with Local Cuisine

Many wine tastings are accompanied by food pairings, allowing visitors to experience the full spectrum of Baden's gastronomic culture. Local dishes such as *Maultaschen* (Swabian dumplings), *Schwarzwälder Schinken* (Black Forest ham), and *Käsespätzle* (cheese noodles) go wonderfully with the wines of the region. Some wineries even offer bespoke tasting menus where each wine is paired with a regional delicacy.

### Wine Events and Festivals

Baden is known for its wine festivals, which offer a unique opportunity to explore the diverse wine offerings of the region. During events such as the *Badischer Weinbautag* or the *Baden Wine Festival*, visitors can participate in tastings directly from the producers, sample local wines, and enjoy live music and entertainment.

## Thermal Spas & Wellness Retreats

### 1. Caracalla Spa (Karlsbad), Baden-Baden

- **Address**: Merkurstraße 3, 76530 Baden-Baden, Germany
- **Opening Hours**: Daily from 8:00 AM to 10:00 PM
- **Price**: Day tickets from €25 for 2 hours; Discounts available for extended stays and packages
- **Facilities**:
    - Indoor and outdoor pools
    - Thermal water pools with varying temperatures
    - Wellness and relaxation areas
    - Sauna village with 11 different saunas
    - Steam baths and steam rooms

- Wellness treatments (massages, facials, etc.)

Located in the spa town of Baden-Baden, Caracalla Spa offers an authentic Roman-style bath experience. The thermal waters here are rich in minerals, known for their therapeutic properties. Whether soaking in the warm mineral baths or enjoying the state-of-the-art sauna village, visitors can experience a true sense of relaxation. The spa also offers wellness treatments, making it a top destination for those seeking both relaxation and health benefits.

## 2. Friedrichsbad (Baden-Baden)

- **Address**: Römerplatz 1, 76530 Baden-Baden, Germany
- **Opening Hours**: Monday to Sunday, 9:00 AM to 10:00 PM
- **Price**: €40 for a standard day pass; Special packages available for additional treatments
- **Facilities**:
    - Roman-Irish bath circuit (thermal baths, steam rooms, and saunas)
    - Relaxation lounges
    - Massages and beauty treatments
    - Traditional bathrobe rentals
    - Historical bath experience

Friedrichsbad is a historic thermal bathhouse in Baden-Baden, combining Roman bath traditions with Irish bathing rituals. It offers a step-by-step bathing ritual, guiding visitors through a sequence of thermal baths, steam rooms, and saunas, allowing them to unwind and detoxify. This elegant spa experience is enhanced by a tranquil atmosphere and historical architecture, making it one of the region's most famous spa destinations.

### 3. Thermen & Badewelt Sinsheim

- **Address**: Badstraße 1, 74889 Sinsheim, Germany
- **Opening Hours**: Monday to Sunday, 9:00 AM to 11:00 PM
- **Price**: Starting at €29 for 2 hours, with discounts for extended stays
- **Facilities**:
    - Large variety of thermal pools
    - Indoor and outdoor areas with warm and hot mineral water
    - Mediterranean-style saunas and wellness area
    - Various beauty and wellness treatments
    - A 300-meter-long water slide and children's pool
    - Salt room and relaxation zones

Thermen & Badewelt Sinsheim is one of the largest and most popular thermal spas in Baden-Württemberg, offering an extensive range of thermal pools and wellness experiences. The large sauna area is particularly notable, featuring saunas from various countries including Finland, Russia, and Turkey. The resort also provides a diverse selection of wellness treatments such as massages, facials, and beauty therapies. Whether you want to relax in a tranquil pool or enjoy an invigorating sauna experience, Sinsheim offers something for everyone.

### 4. Bad Wörishofen Therme

- **Address**: Am Kurpark 4, 86825 Bad Wörishofen, Germany
- **Opening Hours**: Monday to Sunday, 8:00 AM to 9:00 PM
- **Price**: €26 for 3 hours; Special discounts for group bookings and long stays
- **Facilities**:

- Thermal outdoor pools with panoramic views
- Vitality and wellness treatments
- Large sauna village
- Therapeutic mud and mineral baths
- Saltwater pool and floating area

Bad Wörishofen Therme is located in the beautiful Allgäu region and is known for its holistic approach to wellness. The spa's mineral-rich thermal waters are sourced from deep underground springs and are used in various therapeutic treatments. The thermal pools are perfect for unwinding, while the sauna village offers a range of Finnish, infrared, and herbal saunas. This spa retreat is ideal for those seeking a balance of relaxation and therapeutic benefits.

## 5. Solemar Spa (Bad Dürrheim)

- **Address**: Solemarstraße 1, 78073 Bad Dürrheim, Germany
- **Opening Hours**: Monday to Sunday, 9:00 AM to 10:00 PM
- **Price**: Day tickets from €18; Group rates and packages available
- **Facilities**:
    - Saltwater thermal pools
    - Wellness and therapeutic areas
    - Sauna village with several sauna cabins
    - Various relaxation rooms
    - Beauty treatments and massages

Solemar Spa is situated in Bad Dürrheim and is famous for its high-quality saltwater pools. The healing properties of saltwater are central to the spa's philosophy, with guests enjoying the benefits of both relaxation and rejuvenation. The salt-rich air and waters are known for promoting skin health and improving circulation. The wellness center offers a variety of treatments, including salt massages, mud therapies, and holistic wellness packages.

### 6. Bad Mergentheim Therme

- **Address**: Thermenstraße 1, 97980 Bad Mergentheim, Germany
- **Opening Hours**: Monday to Sunday, 9:00 AM to 9:00 PM
- **Price**: €22 for 2 hours; Full-day tickets and wellness packages available
- **Facilities**:
    - Thermal outdoor and indoor pools
    - Extensive sauna areas
    - Various treatments using therapeutic salts and herbs
    - Wellness and spa packages for relaxation and stress relief
    - Beauty and wellness treatments

Located in the scenic town of Bad Mergentheim, this spa offers therapeutic thermal waters and a serene environment for rejuvenation. The wellness center features a large variety of pools, including saltwater baths, and provides multiple saunas and wellness treatments. It is a popular destination for visitors seeking to improve their overall well-being while enjoying the calm atmosphere of the region.

## Folk Music and Dance Performances

### Key Venues for Folk Music and Dance

1. **Baden-Württemberg State Folk Music Ensemble (Staatliche Musikschule)**

- **Address**: Königstraße 36, 70173 Stuttgart, Germany
- **Opening Times**: Monday to Friday, 9 AM - 6 PM
- **Pricing**: Concerts generally range from €15-€30, with discounts for students and seniors.
- **Description**: The Baden-Württemberg State Folk Music Ensemble is dedicated to preserving and showcasing the traditional folk music of the region. They perform at various festivals, public concerts, and private events, often accompanied by folk dances. The ensemble offers a variety of performances, from intimate chamber music settings to larger-scale folk concerts with dancers and singers. Their repertoire includes classic Swabian songs, polkas, and ballads, providing an authentic experience of the region's cultural history.

2. **Swabian-Alemannic Folk Dance Association**
   - **Address**: Haus der Heimat, Albstrasse 52, 70597 Stuttgart, Germany
   - **Opening Times**: Daily, 10 AM - 5 PM (Closed on Sundays)
   - **Pricing**: Entry for folk dance exhibitions is typically €8-€12. Workshops can range from €25-€50.
   - **Description**: A hub for the preservation of Swabian-Alemannic folk dance, this association organizes performances, workshops, and events celebrating regional dances. Traditional dances like the "Schwaben Tanz" (Swabian dance) are performed during cultural events, giving audiences a glimpse of rural traditions that date back hundreds of years. These dances are characterized by their rhythmic movements and the

use of folk costumes, which often tell a story about rural life in the region.

**Folk Festivals and Events**

1. **The Swabian Folk Festival (Schwäbisches Volksfest)**
    - **Location**: Stuttgart, Cannstatter Wasen
    - **Opening Times**: Late April to early May (Exact dates vary each year)
    - **Pricing**: Entrance fees vary, typically €5-€10, with additional charges for special performances or VIP access.
    - **Description**: One of the largest folk festivals in Baden-Württemberg, this event is a celebration of Swabian traditions, including folk music, dancing, and local cuisine. During the festival, traditional Swabian folk bands perform, and dance troupes entertain visitors with colorful, lively dances. The festival offers a true taste of Baden-Württemberg's rural heritage and is an excellent opportunity for tourists to immerse themselves in local culture.

2. **Allemannische Fasnet (Alemannic Carnival)**
    - **Location**: Throughout the region, especially in towns like Rottweil, Villingen, and Tübingen
    - **Opening Times**: February or March (dates vary based on the carnival calendar)
    - **Pricing**: Most events are free to attend, but some special performances or workshops may charge up to €20.
    - **Description**: This carnival, which celebrates the Alemannic traditions of southern Germany, is one of

the most significant events for folk music and dance. The festival includes parades with elaborate masks, traditional drumming, and local folk dances. Participants often perform in traditional costumes, and the accompanying music, such as the distinctive sounds of the "Alphorn" or "Zither," sets a festive mood for the entire region. This carnival represents the deep cultural roots of Baden-Württemberg, showcasing a fusion of music, dance, and folk art.

**Folk Music and Dance in Local Towns**

In many towns across Baden-Württemberg, folk music and dance performances are organized in town squares, during public celebrations, and at cultural venues. These performances are typically free or involve a minimal fee for a more interactive experience. Some of the best places to see these performances include:

- **Freiburg im Breisgau**: Known for its vibrant cultural scene, Freiburg hosts regular folk dance nights where visitors can join in the fun and learn local dance steps.
- **Tübingen**: During summer, the town squares come alive with folk music performances, and local groups often organize spontaneous dance gatherings for tourists and locals alike.

**Workshops and Interactive Experiences**

For those looking to get hands-on, many local folk music schools and cultural centers offer workshops where visitors can try traditional instruments like the "Schwabenflöte" (a type of flute) or learn the basic steps of the regional dances. These workshops are ideal for those wishing to engage more deeply with Baden-Württemberg's cultural fabric.

1. **Folk Dance Workshops at the Swabian Folk Dance Academy**
    - **Address**: Hauptstraße 26, 71522 Backnang, Germany

- **Opening Times**: Weekdays, 9 AM - 7 PM (Closed on Sundays)
- **Pricing**: €25-€50 per workshop
- **Description**: This academy offers hands-on folk dance workshops, where visitors can learn the intricacies of Swabian folk dance. The sessions are led by experienced instructors and often include a performance at the end, allowing participants to showcase their new skills.

2. **Traditional Music Workshops at the Music School of Heidelberg**
   - **Address**: Bergheimer Str. 28, 69115 Heidelberg, Germany
   - **Opening Times**: Monday to Friday, 10 AM - 6 PM
   - **Pricing**: €15-€25 for a session
   - **Description**: The Music School offers opportunities to explore Baden-Württemberg's folk music. Visitors can try out traditional instruments or take part in group singing sessions, immersing themselves in the region's musical heritage.

## Exploring Historic Towns and Villages

### 1. Heidelberg

**Address:** Altstadt (Old Town), Heidelberg, Germany; **Opening Times:** Open year-round; most attractions operate from 9:00 AM - 6:00 PM; **Pricing:** Castle tickets range from €9 to €15 depending on access levels. Museums range from €5 to €12.

Heidelberg is often considered the heart of Baden-Württemberg, where history and culture seamlessly blend into the urban landscape. The highlight of this historic town is **Heidelberg Castle**, perched on the hilltop overlooking the city. The castle's **German Pharmacy Museum** showcases the history of medicine and alchemy, offering an engaging, in-depth cultural experience.

Wander through **Heidelberg's Old Town**, a maze of cobblestone streets with charming buildings, cafes, and shops. Don't miss **Marktplatz**, a vibrant square surrounded by centuries-old architecture. Experience the **Heidelberg University Library**, which is one of the oldest in Germany, offering not just history but also exhibitions related to the city's academic past.

- **Dining:** The **Schnitzelbank** offers authentic Swabian cuisine in the heart of the Old Town, with classics like Maultaschen (Swabian dumplings) and Spätzle (egg noodles).
- **Accommodation: Hotel Villa Marstall**, located near the river and offering views of the castle, provides a blend of historic architecture and modern amenities.

### 2. Freiburg im Breisgau

**Address:** Münsterplatz 1, 79098 Freiburg, Germany; **Opening Times:** Freiburg Cathedral open daily from 10:00 AM - 5:00 PM.; **Pricing:** Free entry to the cathedral; tours available for €6-€8.

Freiburg, with its vibrant student population and proximity to the Black Forest, offers a unique blend of history and nature. The **Freiburg Minster** (Cathedral), with its striking Gothic architecture, towers over the city. Visit the **Augustinermuseum**, housed in a former monastery, to see art collections from the Middle Ages to the 20th century.

Stroll through the **Altstadt (Old Town)**, featuring narrow, winding streets and the iconic **Bächle** (small streams) running along them, a reminder of the city's medieval past. Freiburg is a gateway to the Black

Forest, and hiking trails from the city lead into picturesque natural landscapes.

- **Dining: Gasthaus zum Kranz** serves traditional Swabian fare with a focus on locally sourced ingredients.
- **Accommodation:** For a charming stay, **Hotel Oberkirch** offers a historic location with views of the Münster.

**3. Tübingen**

**Address:** Tübingen, 72070, Germany; **Opening Times:** Year-round, with museums open from 9:00 AM - 5:00 PM; **Pricing:** Museums typically range from €4 to €8 for entry.

Tübingen is a university town brimming with history and academic tradition. The **Hölderlin Tower**, where the famous poet lived, offers a fascinating glimpse into the life of Germany's literary giants. The **Tübingen Castle**, now home to the University Museum, showcases historical artifacts and offers stunning views of the surrounding town and river.

Explore the **Old Town**, with its colorful houses, timber-framed buildings, and narrow alleyways, often compared to a living museum. Take a boat ride on the **Neckar River** with a traditional wooden punt, which offers a peaceful way to admire the town's beauty.

- **Dining: Restaurant Top Cuisines** serves gourmet Swabian dishes, a fusion of modern and traditional flavors.
- **Accommodation: Hotel La Casa**, located near the Old Town, offers boutique-style rooms with access to the main attractions.

**4. Rothenburg ob der Tauber**

**Address:** Rothenburg ob der Tauber, Bavaria, Germany; **Opening Times:** Open year-round with most attractions operating from 10:00

AM - 6:00 PM.; **Pricing:** The **Medieval Crime and Justice Museum** charges an entry fee of €6.

Although technically located in Bavaria, **Rothenburg ob der Tauber** is a must-visit historic town that shares a cultural link with Baden-Württemberg due to its medieval roots. The **Rothenburg Town Walls**, with their well-preserved watchtowers and gates, offer a glimpse into the town's fortified past. The **Plönlein** square, with its iconic half-timbered houses, feels like stepping into a fairy tale.

- **Dining: Gasthof Goldener Greifen** serves hearty German meals in a historic setting.
- **Accommodation:** Stay at **Hotel Eisenhut**, which blends old-world charm with modern comforts.

## 5. Maulbronn

**Address:** Maulbronn Monastery, Kloster Maulbronn, 75433 Maulbronn, Germany; **Opening Times:** Open daily from 9:00 AM - 5:00 PM; **Pricing:** Entry to the monastery costs approximately €7, with guided tours available for an additional €3-€4.

Maulbronn is home to the **Maulbronn Monastery**, a UNESCO World Heritage site and one of the best-preserved medieval monasteries in Europe. The **Monastery's Cloisters** and **Church** provide a stunning backdrop for an immersive historical experience. The surrounding town is equally charming, with its rustic buildings and picturesque countryside.

- **Dining:** The **Klosterstüble** offers a peaceful, rustic setting with regional specialties.
- **Accommodation:** Stay at **Hotel Gasthof zum Bären**, which offers cozy accommodations and is located near the monastery.

# Cooking Classes for Local Specialties

## 1. SchwabenKitchen – Stuttgart

**Address:**; SchwabenKitchen, Königstraße 36, 70173 Stuttgart, Germany

**Opening Times:**; Monday to Saturday: 10:00 AM – 6:00 PM (Private classes available on request)

**Pricing:**; Group classes: €80–€120 per person; Private lessons: €150–€250 per person

SchwabenKitchen offers an authentic experience of Swabian cuisine, a cornerstone of the region's culinary tradition. Guests are led through the preparation of iconic dishes such as **Maultaschen (Swabian Dumplings)** and **Spätzle (Egg Noodles)**, both staples of the local diet. These classes not only teach cooking techniques but also delve into the history and regional variations of each dish.

The instructors, typically local chefs, emphasize using fresh, seasonal ingredients. Participants will also learn about essential local herbs and spices that define Swabian flavors, and at the end of the session, enjoy a communal meal of everything prepared during the class.

**Highlight:** The hands-on nature of the class, coupled with a deep dive into the regional food culture, makes this one of the best experiences for anyone wanting to truly understand the heart of Swabian cuisine.

## 2. Black Forest Cooking School – Freiburg

**Address:**; Black Forest Cooking School, Alter Messplatz 1, 79098 Freiburg, Germany

**Opening Times:**; Wednesday to Sunday: 11:00 AM – 5:00 PM (Pre-booking required)

**Pricing:**; Group classes: €95–€130 per person; Private lessons: €175–€300 per person

The **Black Forest Cooking School** offers an exquisite opportunity to learn how to prepare traditional **Black Forest dishes**, which include hearty, robust meals often made with local meats, fresh produce, and, of course, the famed **Black Forest ham**. The school's specialty is teaching how to create dishes like **Zwiebelrostbraten (Onion Roast)** and **Schwarzwälder Kirschtorte (Black Forest Cake)**.

In these classes, you'll work directly with local ingredients such as wild mushrooms, game meats, and fresh herbs sourced from the Black Forest region. The instructors guide you through the cooking process while sharing local legends and folklore related to the food. The combination of storytelling and cooking offers a truly immersive cultural experience.

**Highlight:** The Black Forest Cake lesson is a must, where participants learn to balance the rich flavors of chocolate, cherries, and whipped cream in the traditional manner.

### 3. Kochschule Tasting – Heidelberg

**Address:**; Kochschule Tasting, Am Hohen Damm 20, 69124 Heidelberg, Germany

**Opening Times:**; Monday to Friday: 9:00 AM – 4:00 PM; Saturday: 10:00 AM – 3:00 PM (Private bookings available)

**Pricing:**; Group classes: €70–€100 per person; Private lessons: €200–€350 per session

In the charming city of Heidelberg, **Kochschule Tasting** specializes in offering cooking classes that focus on the regional dishes from Baden and the surrounding areas. Here, you will master the art of **Käsespätzle (Cheese Noodles)** and **Schupfnudeln (Potato Dumplings)**, two dishes that are beloved throughout the state.

The classes are structured for all skill levels, from beginner to advanced, ensuring that everyone can engage with the recipes and techniques at their own pace. One of the highlights is learning how to make authentic **Flammkuchen**, an Alsatian-style pizza, which is particularly popular in the southwestern regions of Germany. Each class also includes tips on pairing wines from the Baden wine region, enhancing the overall dining experience.

**Highlight:** The emphasis on wine pairing with local dishes makes this class particularly appealing to food and wine lovers.

### 4. Bollenbacher's Cooking Studio – Karlsruhe

**Address:**; Bollenbacher's Cooking Studio, Mühlstraße 4, 76185 Karlsruhe, Germany

**Opening Times:**; Tuesday to Friday: 10:00 AM – 7:00 PM; Saturday: 10:00 AM – 4:00 PM

**Pricing:**; Group classes: €85–€110 per person; Private lessons: €180–€280 per person

**Bollenbacher's Cooking Studio** provides an intimate and personalized cooking experience in the heart of Karlsruhe. Known for its dedication to showcasing Baden-Württemberg's regional cuisine, the studio offers classes focused on **regional seasonal ingredients**, and each session aims to build understanding of the local farming culture.

Dishes such as **Baden-style roasted pork with sauerkraut** and **freshly made potato salad** are taught alongside traditional baking methods for German bread and pastries. The studio also incorporates classes where participants learn the secrets behind some of Baden-Württemberg's classic desserts like **Apfelstrudel** (apple strudel).

**Highlight:** The studio's interactive environment and focus on using local seasonal produce ensure that every dish is prepared with the utmost freshness, making it a favorite for culinary enthusiasts.

### 5. Die Kochfabrik – Stuttgart

**Address:**; Die Kochfabrik, Keplerstraße 4, 70174 Stuttgart, Germany

**Opening Times:**;  Monday to Saturday: 9:30 AM – 6:00 PM (Booking required for evening classes)

**Pricing:**;  Group classes: €80–€120 per person;  Private lessons: €150–€250 per session

**Die Kochfabrik** in Stuttgart provides a modern take on traditional Swabian cooking. Here, participants are introduced to a fusion of modern and classical techniques to create dishes like **Maultaschen** and **Sauerbraten (marinated pot roast)**. The classes focus on teaching not just the recipes but also the techniques that make Swabian food special, such as rolling, stuffing, and braising.

**Highlight:** The hands-on aspect and the stylish, professional kitchen setting make this class an excellent option for those looking to elevate their cooking skills while enjoying a local experience.

# CHAPTER 8.

# NIGHTLIFE & ENTERTAINMENT

## Best Bars & Cocktail Lounges

**1. The Stuttgart Beer Garden**

- **Address:** Schlossplatz 1, 70173 Stuttgart
- **Opening Hours:** Monday–Thursday: 11:00 AM–11:00 PM, Friday–Saturday: 11:00 AM–1:00 AM, Sunday: Closed
- **Pricing:** Beers from €3.50, Cocktails from €7
- **Description:** Located at the heart of Stuttgart, The Stuttgart Beer Garden offers a quintessential German experience with traditional beer options, served in an iconic beer garden atmosphere. It is a favorite among locals and tourists alike. Here, guests can sample locally brewed beer while enjoying traditional Swabian snacks. The venue provides a lively setting with plenty of outdoor seating, perfect for enjoying a warm evening.

**2. Cube Bar**

- **Address:** Eberhardstraße 4, 70173 Stuttgart

- **Opening Hours:** Monday–Thursday: 5:00 PM–1:00 AM, Friday–Saturday: 5:00 PM–3:00 AM, Sunday: Closed
- **Pricing:** Cocktails from €10, Signature Drinks from €12
- **Description:** Situated atop the prestigious Le Meridien Hotel, Cube Bar offers breathtaking panoramic views of Stuttgart's skyline. The sleek, modern interior exudes sophistication, and the cocktail menu reflects a perfect balance of classic concoctions and innovative mixes. Signature drinks such as the "Cube Martini" and "Baden Sour" are crowd favorites. A great spot for sunset drinks or a late-night rendezvous.

### 3. The Botanist

- **Address:** Hauptstraße 73, 69117 Heidelberg
- **Opening Hours:** Monday–Thursday: 6:00 PM–12:00 AM, Friday–Saturday: 6:00 PM–2:00 AM, Sunday: Closed
- **Pricing:** Cocktails from €8, Signature Cocktails from €12
- **Description:** Nestled in the historic town of Heidelberg, The Botanist is known for its herb-infused cocktails and lush, green décor. The venue specializes in botanical cocktails, crafted with fresh herbs and spices to bring unique flavors to every drink. The bar staff takes great pride in their mixology, using a variety of house-made syrups and infusions. It's a cozy, intimate environment perfect for a relaxed evening with friends or a date.

### 4. Die Kutsche

- **Address:** Marktstraße 26, 79098 Freiburg im Breisgau
- **Opening Hours:** Monday–Thursday: 6:00 PM–1:00 AM, Friday–Saturday: 6:00 PM–3:00 AM, Sunday: 6:00 PM–12:00 AM
- **Pricing:** Beers from €3.50, Cocktails from €9

- **Description:** Located in the center of Freiburg, Die Kutsche is one of the city's oldest bars, offering a cozy and rustic charm. The bar features a mix of historical architecture with modern touches, making it an ideal spot for a laid-back night out. The cocktail list is extensive, and regulars rave about the bartender's skill in crafting tailored drinks. The atmosphere is warm and welcoming, making it the perfect place to mingle or enjoy a quiet evening.

## 5. Weinstube Fröhlich

- **Address:** Oberer Wiesenbach 7, 69117 Heidelberg
- **Opening Hours:** Monday–Thursday: 5:00 PM–12:00 AM, Friday–Saturday: 5:00 PM–2:00 AM, Sunday: Closed
- **Pricing:** Wine by the glass from €4.50, Cocktails from €9
- **Description:** For those seeking a more refined experience, Weinstube Fröhlich is the ultimate wine bar in Heidelberg. This quaint spot focuses on providing an extensive selection of wines from the Baden-Württemberg region. The ambiance is intimate, featuring wooden beams and rustic furniture, which complements the impressive list of local and international wines. Though primarily a wine bar, Weinstube Fröhlich also offers expertly mixed cocktails, including wine-based creations that you won't find elsewhere.

## 6. Bar Centrale

- **Address:** Kaiserstraße 72, 76133 Karlsruhe
- **Opening Hours:** Monday–Thursday: 7:00 PM–1:00 AM, Friday–Saturday: 7:00 PM–3:00 AM, Sunday: Closed
- **Pricing:** Cocktails from €7, Wine from €5 per glass
- **Description:** Bar Centrale is a lively yet elegant cocktail bar located in Karlsruhe's central district. Known for its exceptional

service and extensive cocktail menu, this bar offers everything from expertly crafted classics to avant-garde concoctions. The highlight here is the extensive rum collection, which is often incorporated into the bar's signature cocktails. The bar's central location means it's always buzzing with energy, making it a fantastic choice for those seeking a vibrant nightlife experience.

### 7. The Whiskey Meister

- **Address:** Kirchstraße 2, 78462 Konstanz
- **Opening Hours:** Monday–Thursday: 5:00 PM–12:00 AM, Friday–Saturday: 5:00 PM–2:00 AM, Sunday: Closed
- **Pricing:** Whiskey from €5 per shot, Cocktails from €9
- **Description:** Situated by Lake Constance, The Whiskey Meister is the ultimate destination for whiskey lovers. With over 150 types of whiskey available, the bar offers a unique tasting experience that includes both international and local varieties. The staff are incredibly knowledgeable, happy to recommend pairings or guide you through the whiskey-making process. The intimate setting, combined with the unparalleled whiskey collection, makes it the ideal spot for enthusiasts and casual drinkers alike.

### 8. Kesselhaus Bar

- **Address:** Alte Messe 1, 68163 Mannheim
- **Opening Hours:** Monday–Thursday: 6:00 PM–1:00 AM, Friday–Saturday: 6:00 PM–3:00 AM, Sunday: Closed
- **Pricing:** Cocktails from €10, Craft Beers from €5
- **Description:** Kesselhaus Bar is a trendy and industrial-inspired bar in Mannheim, featuring a selection of craft cocktails and locally brewed beers. The venue's minimalist design and

exposed brick walls create a hip ambiance perfect for a night out with friends. The bartenders are skilled in their craft, offering seasonal cocktails and taking pride in creating visually striking presentations. It's a popular spot for young locals and tourists looking for a stylish yet laid-back bar experience.

## Live Music Venues and Concert Halls

**1. Stuttgart State Opera (Staatsoper Stuttgart)**

- **Address:** Oberer Schlossgarten 6, 70173 Stuttgart
- **Opening Times:** Mon-Sat: 10:00 AM - 8:00 PM (Box Office), Shows usually in the evenings starting from 7:00 PM
- **Ticket Prices:** From €20 to €150, depending on the seating and performance
- **Website:** Stuttgart State Opera

As one of the most prestigious opera houses in Germany, the Stuttgart State Opera is renowned for its outstanding acoustics and world-class productions. The venue regularly hosts operas, ballets, and orchestral performances. Its rich history and commitment to presenting classic and contemporary works make it a must-visit for anyone in search of top-tier musical performances.; Apart from opera, the venue also has performances by renowned orchestras and solo concerts by famous artists. It is part of the Stuttgart Cultural Centre, which adds to its accessibility and significance in the city's cultural life.

**2. Porsche Arena**

- **Address:** Mercedesstraße 69, 70372 Stuttgart
- **Opening Times:** Concerts typically start around 8:00 PM
- **Ticket Prices:** From €40 to €150, depending on the artist
- **Website:** Porsche Arena Stuttgart

The Porsche Arena is one of the largest and most versatile venues in Baden-Württemberg, hosting a wide range of events, including live music performances by global artists, pop concerts, rock bands, and even electronic dance music events. Its modern design and superior acoustics create an immersive experience for both performers and audiences.; With a capacity of around 7,000, the arena attracts major international stars across multiple genres, from classical music to contemporary and electronic performances.

**3. Jazzclub Bix Stuttgart**

- **Address:** Ecke Beethovenstraße / Tübinger Str., 70199 Stuttgart
- **Opening Times:** Tues-Sun: 7:00 PM - 2:00 AM
- **Ticket Prices:** €15 to €30
- **Website:** Jazzclub Bix

For fans of jazz, Bix Stuttgart offers an intimate setting for enjoying live performances in one of the city's most iconic venues. Since opening in 1999, it has become a hub for jazz lovers, featuring performances from local talents as well as international jazz stars.; The club's interior is cozy and stylish, with excellent acoustics, making it an ideal location for both relaxed evenings and more vibrant music nights. In addition to jazz, the venue also hosts blues, soul, and swing performances, contributing to Stuttgart's rich live music scene.

**4. LKA Longhorn Stuttgart**

- **Address:** Heimstraße 31, 70372 Stuttgart
- **Opening Times:** Concerts and events typically held in the evenings from 7:30 PM onward
- **Ticket Prices:** €20 to €50, varying by artist and event
- **Website:** LKA Longhorn

LKA Longhorn is one of the prime live music venues for rock and alternative music in Stuttgart. Known for hosting some of the biggest names in rock, metal, and indie, this venue provides an immersive concert experience with its strong acoustics and high-energy environment. It has a capacity of around 2,000, creating an up-close and personal atmosphere.; Fans of heavy metal, punk, and hard rock will especially enjoy the venue, but the stage also occasionally welcomes international pop and indie acts.

## 5. Freiburg Concert Hall (Konzerthaus Freiburg)

- **Address:** Platz der Alten Synagoge, 79098 Freiburg
- **Opening Times:** Mon-Sat: 10:00 AM - 6:00 PM (Box Office), Concerts in the evenings from 7:00 PM
- **Ticket Prices:** From €20 to €70
- **Website:** Konzerthaus Freiburg

For a more classical experience, the Freiburg Concert Hall is an exceptional venue with a long-standing tradition of excellent acoustics and a rich history. The hall hosts a variety of performances, including orchestral concerts, chamber music, and recitals. With its elegant design and intimate feel, the Konzerthaus Freiburg offers a more serene, sophisticated experience compared to larger arenas.; The venue is also home to the renowned Freiburg Philharmonic Orchestra, and its varied programming includes performances from some of the world's finest orchestras and soloists.

## 6. 7er Club (Heidelberg)

- **Address:** Willy-Brandt-Platz 1, 69115 Heidelberg
- **Opening Times:** Open daily from 9:00 PM - 4:00 AM
- **Ticket Prices:** Entry typically €10 to €20
- **Website:** 7er Club

In Heidelberg, the 7er Club is the go-to place for live music lovers seeking something more underground. Known for its rock, punk, and indie performances, the club has an intimate, energetic atmosphere that attracts young crowds and offers a chance to see emerging local bands and international acts.; This venue is a staple of Heidelberg's alternative music scene and frequently features experimental music genres, making it a great option for those looking to experience something different.

**7. Jazzhaus Freiburg**

- **Address:** Marienstraße 12, 79098 Freiburg
- **Opening Times:** Mon-Sun: 7:00 PM - 2:00 AM
- **Ticket Prices:** €10 to €35
- **Website:** Jazzhaus Freiburg

As a top destination for jazz lovers, the Jazzhaus in Freiburg is a well-known hotspot for intimate, up-close performances. This venue hosts jazz, blues, soul, and funk performances regularly. It has a relaxed vibe and excellent acoustics, making it a favorite among locals and tourists alike.; The venue also serves as a hub for live music workshops, jam sessions, and smaller concerts, providing an opportunity for both professional and amateur musicians to connect with audiences.

## Theaters, Opera Houses & Performing Arts

**Stuttgart State Theatre (Staatsoper Stuttgart)**

- **Address:** Oberer Wasserturm, 70173 Stuttgart
- **Opening Times:** Performances typically run Tuesday to Saturday, with occasional Sunday performances. Shows begin at 7:00 PM, with matinees on weekends at 4:00 PM.

- **Ticket Prices:** Range from €20 to €180, depending on the performance and seating.
- **Booking:** Tickets available online or at the box office.

Stuttgart State Theatre is one of the premier cultural landmarks in the city, offering a diverse program of opera, ballet, and drama. As one of Germany's oldest and most respected opera houses, it features productions by internationally renowned directors and conductors. The theatre hosts a variety of performances, including classical works by Wagner, Mozart, and Verdi, as well as contemporary pieces. With its striking modernist architecture, the theatre also offers a unique acoustical experience, making it a must-see for lovers of the performing arts.

## National Theatre Mannheim (Nationaltheater Mannheim)

- **Address:** Mozartstr. 9-13, 68161 Mannheim
- **Opening Times:** Performances take place from Wednesday to Sunday, with shows starting at 7:30 PM.
- **Ticket Prices:** Tickets range from €10 to €60, depending on the type of performance and seating. Discounts available for students and seniors.
- **Booking:** Tickets can be purchased online or at the theatre box office.

National Theatre Mannheim is one of the most influential theatres in the region, with a rich tradition dating back to the 18th century. It offers a broad range of productions, from classic theatre works to innovative modern pieces. The theatre has earned a reputation for its bold approach to both classic and experimental theater, regularly staging groundbreaking performances and collaborative international projects. Visitors can enjoy anything from Shakespeare's classics to avant-garde plays by emerging writers.

### Baden State Theatre Karlsruhe (Badisches Staatstheater Karlsruhe)

- **Address:** Kaiserallee 11, 76133 Karlsruhe
- **Opening Times:** Performances typically occur Monday through Saturday at 7:30 PM, with afternoon performances on Sundays at 3:00 PM.
- **Ticket Prices:** Prices range from €18 to €80, with discounted rates available for students.
- **Booking:** Tickets available through the theatre's website or at the box office.

Karlsruhe's Baden State Theatre is a prominent cultural institution with a deep commitment to classical and contemporary theatre, opera, and ballet. It offers a wide array of performances, including traditional operas by composers like Bizet and Puccini, as well as modern works. With its beautifully restored historic building, the theatre combines the grandeur of the past with the innovation of contemporary performances. It's an excellent venue for those interested in classical music and opera, as well as avant-garde productions.

### Freiburg Theatre (Theater Freiburg)

- **Address:** Schiffstr. 1, 79098 Freiburg
- **Opening Times:** Performances typically take place Wednesday through Saturday at 8:00 PM, with some Sunday shows at 5:00 PM.
- **Ticket Prices:** Tickets range from €12 to €40, with various discounts available.
- **Booking:** Tickets can be purchased online or at the box office.

Freiburg Theatre is known for its innovative programming and intimate atmosphere. It presents a wide range of productions, from contemporary theatre to traditional performances, and is particularly famous for its experimental work. With a strong focus on community engagement, Freiburg Theatre regularly hosts local collaborations and performances that address social and political issues. It's also known for its interdisciplinary approach, mixing theatre with visual arts, music, and dance.

**Opera House Freiburg (Opernhaus Freiburg)**

- **Address:** Kaiser-Joseph-Str. 175, 79098 Freiburg
- **Opening Times:** Opera performances typically take place Tuesday through Saturday at 7:30 PM.
- **Ticket Prices:** Prices range from €25 to €100, depending on the opera and seating preference.
- **Booking:** Tickets available through the official website or at the box office.

The Opera House in Freiburg is a focal point of the city's vibrant cultural life. Known for its exceptional acoustics and stunning architecture, it presents an exciting mix of classic and contemporary operas. The venue has hosted internationally acclaimed productions, ranging from the great operas of Verdi and Mozart to modern and experimental works. A visit here provides an immersive experience for opera lovers, with performances staged in a historic yet modern setting.

**The Stuttgart Ballet**

- **Address:** Stuttgart State Theatre, Oberer Wasserturm, 70173 Stuttgart
- **Opening Times:** Performances are typically held from Tuesday to Saturday at 7:30 PM, with matinee shows on Sundays.
- **Ticket Prices:** Ranges from €25 to €150.
- **Booking:** Tickets available online or via the Stuttgart State Theatre's box office.

Stuttgart Ballet is one of the most renowned ballet companies in the world, acclaimed for its technical precision and artistic excellence. Known for its performance of classical ballets by choreographers such as John Cranko, the company is also famous for its contemporary dance productions. The company's repertoire blends traditional ballet with avant-garde works, making it an essential experience for dance enthusiasts.

## Casinos and Late-Night Entertainment

**Casino Stuttgart**

**Address:** Mercedesstraße 30, 70372 Stuttgart; **Opening Times:**

- Sunday to Thursday: 2:00 PM – 3:00 AM
- Friday & Saturday: 2:00 PM – 5:00 AM; **Entry Fee:** Free for most areas; entry to gaming rooms may require a membership or fee.; **Website:** www.casino-stuttgart.de

One of the largest and most sophisticated casinos in Baden-Württemberg, Casino Stuttgart offers an exciting blend of traditional gaming and modern entertainment. Located in the heart of Stuttgart, it features a wide array of games including poker, blackjack, and roulette. The casino's elegantly designed interiors create a classy atmosphere, perfect for high-stakes gaming or simply enjoying the vibrant nightlife.

The venue also offers live entertainment, ranging from DJs to live bands, as well as a chic bar with an extensive cocktail menu. The casino has a fine-dining restaurant, "Le Bistro," offering French-inspired cuisine, making it a great place for a night out, whether you're there for the games or the entertainment.

**Casino Konstanz**

**Address:** Auf der Insel 1, 78462 Konstanz; **Opening Times:**

- Sunday to Thursday: 2:00 PM – 2:00 AM
- Friday & Saturday: 2:00 PM – 4:00 AM; **Entry Fee:** Entry is free for all guests; games require purchase of chips.; **Website:** www.casino-konstanz.de

Set on the picturesque shores of Lake Constance, Casino Konstanz blends stunning views with thrilling gaming options. This mid-sized casino is particularly popular for its relaxed atmosphere, making it ideal for casual gamers and experienced players alike. Guests can try their hand at classic table games like roulette, blackjack, and poker, or enjoy one of the many slot machines available.

Konstanz also offers a comfortable lounge and bar area, where guests can unwind with a cocktail while enjoying the serene lakeside setting. The casino occasionally hosts themed events and live music, creating a lively environment into the early hours of the morning.

**Casino Baden-Baden**

**Address:** Kaiserallee 1, 76530 Baden-Baden; **Opening Times:**

- Sunday to Thursday: 2:00 PM – 3:00 AM
- Friday & Saturday: 2:00 PM – 5:00 AM; **Entry Fee:** €5 entry; €10 for special events.; **Website:** www.casino-baden-baden.de

Known for its historical charm, Casino Baden-Baden is one of the most renowned casinos in Germany. Located in the world-famous spa town of Baden Baden, the casino is housed in a beautiful 19th century building. The casino is famous for its opulent design, reminiscent of a royal palace, and offers an elegant and sophisticated gaming experience.

The casino features a variety of games, including several tables for roulette, blackjack, and poker. Visitors can also enjoy a range of slot machines. Besides gaming, Casino Baden-Baden is known for its high-quality dining options, with a gourmet restaurant offering exquisite French and international cuisine. The casino regularly hosts live music performances, adding to the venue's upscale appeal.

**Late-Night Entertainment in Stuttgart**

Stuttgart is known for its dynamic nightlife, offering everything from late-night bars to clubs and live music venues. Many of the city's bars stay open until the early hours, with some offering live DJ performances and dance floors. Here are a few recommendations:

**The Longhorn Café**; **Address:** Heusteigstraße 44, 70180 Stuttgart; **Opening Times:** 6:00 PM – 4:00 AM (daily); The Longhorn Café is a popular choice for those who enjoy live country music and a Western atmosphere. With its rustic décor, it offers a warm and friendly ambiance for those who want to dance or simply enjoy the music.

**Climax Institutes**; **Address:** Tübinger Str. 15, 70178 Stuttgart; **Opening Times:** 10:00 PM – 5:00 AM (Thursday to Saturday); A top destination for electronic dance music enthusiasts, Climax Institutes hosts some of the best techno, house, and trance DJs from around the world. With its impressive sound system and great vibe, it's a must-visit for fans of electronic music.

**SchwabenQuellen**; **Address:** Krailenshaldenstraße 24, 70599 Stuttgart; **Opening Times:** Open until midnight (daily); For a more relaxing but still vibrant experience, SchwabenQuellen is a unique venue where visitors can enjoy late-night spa experiences. Offering a range of themed saunas and wellness treatments, SchwabenQuellen also features several bars and lounges, where guests can unwind and sip cocktails.

**Late-Night Bars and Lounges**

For those who prefer a more relaxed late-night experience, there are plenty of chic bars in cities like Stuttgart, Freiburg, and Heidelberg that stay open late into the night. Some top spots include:

- **Kleine Bar Stuttgart** – A cozy cocktail bar with an intimate atmosphere and an excellent selection of drinks, located at Rotebühlplatz.
- **Balthasar Bar Freiburg** – This sophisticated, upscale bar offers a wide range of cocktails, liquors, and spirits, with an atmosphere that encourages conversation and relaxation.

# CHAPTER 9.

# SHOPPING & SOUVENIRS

## High-End Shopping Streets & Malls

**Stuttgart: Königstraße and The Köngen Outlet City**

**Address:**; Königstraße, 70173 Stuttgart, Germany

**Opening Times:**

- Monday to Saturday: 10:00 AM – 8:00 PM
- Closed on Sundays

Königstraße is Stuttgart's central shopping street and one of the longest pedestrian zones in Europe. Spanning from the central train station (Hauptbahnhof) through the heart of the city, this street boasts a mix of luxury boutiques, department stores, and high-end fashion outlets.

Among the most sought-after brands, you'll find flagship stores such as Louis Vuitton, Hugo Boss, and Prada. The street also hosts exclusive jewelry stores like Tiffany & Co. and Cartier, making it a true hub for luxury shopping. In addition to these, several upscale department stores like Breuninger offer a curated collection of high-end fashion, cosmetics, and lifestyle products.

For a more niche experience, check out some of the smaller boutiques tucked along the side streets, offering rare European and international fashion labels, as well as high-quality German-made leather goods.

For a truly exclusive outlet experience, head to **Outletcity Metzingen**, just a short drive from Stuttgart. Located in the charming town of Metzingen, this outlet mall offers discounted items from top-tier brands like Burberry, Dolce & Gabbana, and Michael Kors. With over 70 outlets, it's perfect for savvy shoppers looking for both luxury goods and designer deals.

**Heidelberg: Hauptstraße**

**Address:**;  Hauptstraße, 69117 Heidelberg, Germany

**Opening Times:**

- Monday to Saturday: 9:30 AM – 7:00 PM
- Closed on Sundays

Heidelberg's Hauptstraße is a historic and vibrant street lined with a mix of luxurious boutiques and exclusive high-end stores. Known for its academic atmosphere due to the nearby university, this shopping street balances tradition with modernity.

In addition to a variety of high-end fashion outlets, you'll find stores selling sophisticated leather goods and artisan jewelry, such as those offered by **Hugo Boss** and **Loewe**. Notably, the street also includes many designer shoe stores, with international names like **Christian Louboutin** and **Jimmy Choo** represented here.

For those interested in regional specialties, you can find stores featuring exclusive **Swabian artisanal goods**, perfect for gifts or souvenirs.

**Freiburg: Kaiser-Joseph-Straße**

**Address:**;  Kaiser-Joseph-Straße, 79098 Freiburg im Breisgau, Germany

**Opening Times:**
- Monday to Saturday: 10:00 AM – 6:00 PM
- Closed on Sundays

Freiburg's shopping scene is elevated on Kaiser-Joseph-Straße, the city's primary shopping area. While the street itself exudes a charming medieval atmosphere, it is home to several designer boutiques and high-end fashion stores. Labels like **Lacoste** and **Ralph Lauren** are represented here, catering to shoppers with refined tastes.

Moreover, the street is also home to **luxury jewelry boutiques** that feature pieces from local and international jewelers. Expect to see everything from classic designs to contemporary pieces made with precious stones and metals.

For a truly unique shopping experience, Freiburg is also known for its specialty stores selling artisanal and handcrafted products, such as handmade shoes and bags crafted by local designers, allowing visitors to take home a piece of the region's craftsmanship.

**Karlsruhe: Ettlinger Tor Galerie**

**Address:**; Ettlinger Tor Galerie, Kaiserstraße 120, 76133 Karlsruhe, Germany

**Opening Times:**
- Monday to Saturday: 10:00 AM – 8:00 PM
- Closed on Sundays

The Ettlinger Tor Galerie in Karlsruhe is a stylish and modern shopping center that offers a mix of luxury and contemporary shopping experiences. The mall houses **international high-end brands** such as **Gucci**, **Armani**, and **Salvatore Ferragamo**, alongside popular fashion chains and local boutiques.

With more than 70 shops spread across three levels, it caters to a wide range of shoppers, including those seeking both luxury items and trendy streetwear. The mall also features **exclusive German cosmetics** and skincare lines, providing a holistic experience for those looking to pamper themselves.

Additionally, the Ettlinger Tor Galerie boasts a selection of **local handcrafted gifts and souvenirs**, from fine ceramic works to delicate wood carvings, which make for unique and meaningful mementos of your trip.

**Shopping in Baden-Württemberg: More Luxurious Locations**

1. **Baden-Baden:**; Known as the "Monte Carlo of Germany," Baden-Baden offers elegant boutiques and designer stores like **Chanel**, **Fendi**, and **Louis Vuitton** along its **Lichtentaler Allee** and **Gernsbacher Straße**. These areas provide a high-end shopping experience, nestled in the city's historic spa town charm.

2. **Pforzheim:**; Pforzheim is renowned for its fine jewelry and watchmaking heritage. The city is home to several luxury jewelry boutiques and artisan stores selling meticulously crafted pieces from local designers, perfect for those seeking something exclusive and high-quality.

## Local Markets and Artisan Crafts

**1. Stuttgart's Farmers' Market (Stuttgarter Wochenmarkt)**

- **Address:** Marktplatz, 70173 Stuttgart
- **Opening Times:** Monday to Friday: 7:00 AM - 4:00 PM, Saturday: 7:00 AM - 1:00 PM
- **Pricing:** Varies depending on products, with fresh produce and regional goods starting at €1–€10

Stuttgart's Farmers' Market, held in the heart of the city at Marktplatz, is an excellent destination for shoppers seeking fresh, locally sourced food and artisanal goods. The market features an array of stalls offering everything from fresh fruits, vegetables, and cheeses to homemade breads, cured meats, and seasonal specialties. A must-visit for food lovers, the market is a hub for local farmers and food producers, making it the perfect spot to pick up edible souvenirs like Black Forest ham, Swabian mustard, or honey from regional hives.

Shoppers can also find handcrafted wooden items, fresh flowers, and regional wine from nearby vineyards. Prices are fair and reflect the high quality of the local produce and goods. For those looking for something truly special, the market's artisans often sell beautiful handcrafted wooden toys, kitchenware, and textiles made from locally sourced materials.

**2. Freiburg's Munsterplatz Market**

- **Address:** Munsterplatz, 79098 Freiburg
- **Opening Times:** Monday to Saturday: 7:00 AM - 1:00 PM
- **Pricing:** Handcrafted goods typically range from €5–€30, depending on the item

Located in the vibrant historic center of Freiburg, the Munsterplatz market is one of the oldest and most popular in the region. Situated near the Freiburg Minster Cathedral, this open-air market is known for its colorful stalls filled with artisanal crafts, local produce, and handmade goods. It's an ideal place to explore if you are looking for authentic souvenirs with a strong regional flair.

Shoppers can find intricately crafted Black Forest cuckoo clocks, hand-carved wooden figurines, and intricate lacework. For those with a taste for art, local painters often sell their paintings and prints depicting scenes from the Black Forest and Freiburg's charming streets. The prices vary depending on the craftsmanship, but customers can find affordable trinkets as well as high-end collectible pieces.

### 3. The Heilbronn Market (Heilbronner Wochenmarkt)

- **Address:** Allee, 74072 Heilbronn
- **Opening Times:** Tuesday and Friday: 7:00 AM - 1:00 PM
- **Pricing:** Local products such as honey, preserves, and sausages range from €5–€15

The Heilbronn Market offers a wonderful selection of traditional Swabian foods and local crafts. Located in the heart of Heilbronn, this market is especially renowned for its fresh, locally grown produce and specialty foods, such as the region's famous Swabian pretzels and artisanal cheeses.

Beyond food, shoppers can also find high-quality pottery and hand-painted ceramics crafted by local artisans. Traditional wooden toys and cutting boards, carved from locally sourced timber, are also popular items among tourists. The market's affordable prices make it an excellent spot for souvenir hunting, especially for those looking for practical yet unique gifts.

### 4. Nuremberg Christmas Market (Christkindlesmarkt)

- **Address:** Hauptmarkt, 90403 Nuremberg (Near Baden-Württemberg)
- **Opening Times:** Late November to Christmas Eve: 10:00 AM - 9:00 PM
- **Pricing:** Souvenirs typically range from €2–€30

Although not strictly within Baden-Württemberg, the Nuremberg Christmas Market is a short trip from the region and offers a magical shopping experience during the holiday season. Known worldwide for its festive atmosphere, this market features over 180 stalls that sell a variety of Christmas-themed handcrafted items, including hand-carved wooden ornaments, delicate glass decorations, and intricate gingerbread cookies.

For those interested in holiday shopping, Nuremberg's Christmas Market is a treasure trove of artisanal goods that embody the spirit of the season. While the prices may be higher due to the festive nature of the market, shoppers will find plenty of items that make for cherished gifts or keepsakes from their visit to the region.

**5. Boutique Shops in Tübingen**

- **Address:** Untere Wässere, 72072 Tübingen
- **Opening Times:** Monday to Saturday: 10:00 AM - 6:00 PM
- **Pricing:** Handcrafted items range from €10–€50

The university town of Tübingen is home to a number of charming boutiques that specialize in local crafts and high-quality fashion. While strolling along the picturesque streets, visitors can find handmade leather goods such as wallets, belts, and bags, as well as artisanal jewelry created by local designers. These boutiques offer an excellent selection of gifts for those interested in something more sophisticated than traditional souvenirs.

In addition, Tübingen's shops feature unique home décor items like handwoven rugs and decorative pottery, many of which are made by regional artisans. Prices are moderate, making it a great place to pick up something stylish and locally produced.

**6. Black Forest Crafts**

- **Address:** Various locations, including Triberg and Baden-Baden
- **Opening Times:** Varies by location; generally open daily from 10:00 AM - 6:00 PM
- **Pricing:** Prices for handcrafted wooden items and cuckoo clocks range from €20–€200

The Black Forest (Schwarzwald) region is famous for its high-quality wooden products, including the iconic cuckoo clocks that the area has been known for centuries. In towns like Triberg and Baden-Baden, visitors will find workshops and galleries selling these timepieces, often crafted by hand using traditional techniques passed down through generations. The clocks are available in a wide range of styles, from simple and rustic to intricate and ornate, allowing shoppers to find something that fits their taste and budget.

Beyond cuckoo clocks, the Black Forest region is known for its expertly crafted wooden toys, figurines, and kitchenware. These artisanal pieces are perfect souvenirs for anyone looking for a functional yet beautiful keepsake from the area.

**7. Local Vineyards and Wine Shops**

- **Address:** Various vineyards across the Baden region
- **Opening Times:** Varies by vineyard, generally 10:00 AM - 5:00 PM
- **Pricing:** Wine bottles range from €10–€50, with some premium wines costing more

For wine lovers, Baden-Württemberg is home to several renowned wine regions, including the Baden wine region, known for its pinot noir and riesling varieties. Visitors can tour vineyards and purchase wines directly from local producers. Many vineyards offer guided tours where you can sample different varieties and learn about the winemaking process, making it a great opportunity to take home a bottle (or several) as a unique and authentic souvenir.

In addition to wine, many of the vineyards also sell wine-related accessories, such as hand-blown glassware, wine stoppers, and locally produced grape-based products like jams and vinegars.

# Best Places for Black Forest Cuckoo Clocks

### 1. The Cuckoo Clock Museum in Triberg

- **Address:**; Vogtstraße 41, 78098 Triberg im Schwarzwald, Germany
- **Opening Hours:**; Daily, 9:00 AM – 6:00 PM
- **Pricing:**; Adults: €7.50, Children (6-12 years): €3.50, Family ticket: €18.00
- **Special Information:**; The museum houses one of the largest collections of cuckoo clocks in the world, offering visitors an immersive experience into the history and artistry behind these beloved timepieces. You can witness the entire process of cuckoo clock creation and even see clocks from the 18th century. The museum shop features a broad range of clocks, from classic to modern designs, made by local artisans.

The Cuckoo Clock Museum in Triberg is an absolute must for any serious cuckoo clock enthusiast. Triberg itself is a central hub for the region's clock-making heritage, and this museum brings the story of the Black Forest clocks to life. Whether you're looking for a traditional cuckoo clock or a more contemporary design, the museum's on-site shop ensures that you find a piece that suits your needs.

### 2. Schmidt's Cuckoo Clock Shop

- **Address:**; Hauptstraße 12, 78144 Schiltach, Germany
- **Opening Hours:**; Monday – Saturday: 9:00 AM – 5:00 PM, Sunday: Closed
- **Pricing:**; Prices for clocks range from €200 to over €2,000 depending on the design and craftsmanship.

- **Special Information:**; Schmidt's Cuckoo Clock Shop is known for offering some of the finest handcrafted cuckoo clocks in the region. This family-run business has been a staple in Schiltach for generations and provides a wide selection of clocks, from small, classic models to large, ornately carved timepieces. Visitors can expect to find a detailed selection of hand-carved wooden clocks, as well as modern variations. Expert staff are available to provide personalized advice and guidance, helping you choose the perfect clock that matches your home or collection.

This shop offers an authentic experience, with the opportunity to meet the artisans who craft the clocks. It's a great spot to see the precision and care that goes into each piece.

## 3. The House of Black Forest Cuckoo Clocks (Haus der Kuckucksuhren)

- **Address:**; Hauptstraße 48, 77793 Gutach, Germany
- **Opening Hours:**; Monday – Saturday: 9:00 AM – 6:00 PM, Sunday: 10:00 AM – 5:00 PM
- **Pricing:**; Clocks start from approximately €150 for smaller designs, with larger clocks priced upwards of €2,000.
- **Special Information:**; The House of Black Forest Cuckoo Clocks is located in Gutach, a small town at the heart of the Black Forest. Known for its authentic traditional cuckoo clocks, this store offers an extensive range of clocks, from the classic wooden models to more decorative ones featuring elaborate carvings. In addition to purchasing clocks, the museum part of the store offers visitors an educational experience, where you can learn about the history of cuckoo clocks and their influence on the region.

The shop also specializes in providing service and restoration for cuckoo clocks, offering repair services if you need to maintain your clock after purchase. The showroom features pieces from some of the most renowned local clockmakers, giving you a chance to select from a broad selection of quality clocks.

**4. Kuckucksuhren Müller**

- **Address:**;  Brunnengasse 7, 77723 Gengenbach, Germany
- **Opening Hours:**;  Monday – Saturday: 10:00 AM – 5:30 PM, Sunday: Closed
- **Pricing:**;  Prices range from €180 to €3,500, depending on size and craftsmanship.
- **Special Information:**;  Kuckucksuhren Müller is known for its custom-designed cuckoo clocks and personalized engraving options. The store offers a mix of traditional clocks and newer, more innovative designs. If you're looking for something truly unique, this shop offers the option to have your clock engraved with personal messages or dates, perfect for a special gift or milestone.

Kuckucksuhren Müller is renowned for producing a wide range of clocks, including the more elaborate "musical" cuckoo clocks, which not only cuckoo but also play tunes. Whether you are looking for a souvenir for a loved one or a clock for your own home, the store provides an unforgettable shopping experience in the heart of Gengenbach.

**5. Kuckoo Clock Village (Kuckucksuhren-Dorf) in Schonach**

- **Address:**;  Vogtstraße 40, 78136 Schonach im Schwarzwald, Germany
- **Opening Hours:**;  Monday – Saturday: 9:30 AM – 5:30 PM, Sunday: 10:00 AM – 4:00 PM

- **Pricing:**; Prices for cuckoo clocks start at €250, with some premium models going well beyond €3,000.
- **Special Information:**; The Kuckucksuhrendorf (Cuckoo Clock Village) in Schonach is a delightful destination for cuckoo clock fans. The village itself is home to several clockmakers, each with their own workshops and showrooms. Visitors can purchase directly from the makers, ensuring they get an authentic and quality product. Additionally, the village offers interactive displays where you can see clock-making demonstrations.

The village is also home to an impressive clock tower that showcases one of the largest cuckoo clocks in the world. A visit here offers not only a chance to purchase a clock but also the experience of seeing how these clocks are crafted.

## Traditional Souvenirs & Where to Buy Them

### 1. Black Forest Cuckoo Clocks

Arguably the most iconic souvenir from Baden-Württemberg, cuckoo clocks have a long-standing tradition in the Black Forest (Schwarzwald). These intricately designed clocks are not just functional but also pieces of art.

- **Where to Buy:**
  - *Schwarzwaldhaus*: Located in the heart of the Black Forest region, this is one of the best places to find authentic cuckoo clocks. It's a family-owned shop that has been in operation for over 150 years.
    - **Address:** Schwarzwaldhaus 186, 72250 Freudenstadt, Germany

- **Opening Times:** Monday to Saturday, 9:00 AM – 5:00 PM
- **Prices:** Starting from €100 for smaller models; custom or larger models can range from €300 to over €1,000.
- **Tips:** Be sure to check the craftsmanship of the clock and whether it's handcrafted. Most high-quality cuckoo clocks come with a certificate of authenticity, guaranteeing they are made in the Black Forest region.

**2. Swabian Pottery**

The Swabian region has a rich tradition of pottery making, with handmade ceramics that come in a variety of forms, from decorative pieces to functional tableware. The colorful designs and high-quality craftsmanship make Swabian pottery a beloved souvenir.

- **Where to Buy:**
    - *Keramikmuseum Staufen*: Situated in the charming town of Staufen, this museum showcases a wide variety of local pottery and offers an excellent selection of pieces for purchase.
        - **Address:** Vorstadt 29, 79219 Staufen im Breisgau, Germany
        - **Opening Times:** Monday to Friday, 10:00 AM – 6:00 PM, Saturday 10:00 AM – 4:00 PM
        - **Prices:** Small pieces start from €10, with larger, intricately designed items priced between €50 and €150.
- **Tips:** Look for the signature "Swabian style" which often incorporates earthy tones and rustic designs. Many of these pieces can be personalized, making them even more unique.

**3. Baden Wine**

Baden-Württemberg is one of Germany's prime wine-producing regions, with Baden being particularly famous for its exceptional wine. Local wines, especially the Pinot Noir (Spätburgunder) and Riesling varieties, make for a memorable gift.

- **Where to Buy:**
    - *Weingut Schloss Neuweier*: A renowned wine estate in the Baden region known for its wine production and wine shop.
        - **Address:** Schloss Neuweier, 76530 Baden-Baden, Germany
        - **Opening Times:** Monday to Saturday, 10:00 AM – 6:00 PM
        - **Prices:** Bottles of wine range from €10 to €30, with premium wines priced higher.
- **Tips:** Ask for local recommendations from the wine producers to explore unique, smaller batch wines. The wine shops often offer guided tastings, which can help you make the perfect selection.

**4. Swabian Wooden Toys**

Handcrafted wooden toys are another traditional souvenir from Baden-Württemberg. The region is known for its finely crafted toys made from local wood, often painted with bright, cheerful colors. These toys are perfect for children or anyone who appreciates handmade craftsmanship.

- **Where to Buy:**
    - *Steiff Museum Shop*: Known worldwide for its iconic teddy bears, the Steiff Museum in Giengen offers a variety of high-quality wooden toys, some designed in collaboration with famous toy makers.

- **Address:** Tarzanstraße 10, 89537 Giengen an der Brenz, Germany
- **Opening Times:** Monday to Friday, 10:00 AM – 5:00 PM
- **Prices:** Wooden toys range from €20 to €50 depending on size and design.
- **Tips:** These wooden toys make great nostalgic gifts, and many stores allow you to customize them with names or dates.

## 5. Black Forest Ham

This iconic cured meat from the Black Forest region is known for its smoky, flavorful taste. It's an excellent gift for those who enjoy savory treats, and you can find it in many delicatessens across the region.

- **Where to Buy:**
    - *Haus der Schwarzwälder Schinken*: A specialty store in the heart of the Black Forest dedicated to selling locally produced Black Forest ham.
        - **Address:** Hauptstraße 45, 79822 Titisee-Neustadt, Germany
        - **Opening Times:** Monday to Saturday, 9:00 AM – 6:00 PM
        - **Prices:** A portion of Black Forest ham starts at around €15 per kilogram.
- **Tips:** While in the area, consider buying a variety of smoked meats, as they complement the ham and make for a distinctive culinary gift.

## 6. Local Wine Glasses & Glassware

Baden-Württemberg is also known for its glass-making tradition. Local workshops produce beautiful glassware, including delicate wine glasses, vases, and decorative pieces, perfect for collectors.

- **Where to Buy:**

- *Glasmuseum Epfendorf*: A museum and shop dedicated to the region's glassmaking history.
    - **Address:** Hauptstraße 36, 78736 Epfendorf, Germany
    - **Opening Times:** Tuesday to Saturday, 10:00 AM – 5:00 PM
    - **Prices:** Glassware starts from €15 for smaller items, with more intricate designs costing up to €100 or more.
- **Tips:** Glassware from this region is known for its clarity and craftsmanship. If you're looking for unique pieces, be sure to look for hand-blown glass, as these items are truly one-of-a-kind.

# 7. Local Handicrafts and Art

If you're looking for something truly unique, Baden-Württemberg is home to many artists who create stunning handicrafts, from paintings and sculptures to handwoven textiles. These artistic pieces are perfect souvenirs for anyone interested in supporting local artisans.

- **Where to Buy:**
    - *Kunsthalle Tübingen*: A renowned art gallery where visitors can also purchase works from local artists.
        - **Address:** Wilhelmstraße 123, 72074 Tübingen, Germany
        - **Opening Times:** Tuesday to Sunday, 10:00 AM – 6:00 PM
        - **Prices:** Prices vary significantly based on the artist and type of artwork, but expect to pay anywhere from €50 for smaller pieces to several hundred for larger works.

# CHAPTER 10.

# PRACTICAL INFORMATION

## Currency, ATMs & Payment Options

### Currency and Exchange Rates

Baden-Württemberg, like the rest of Germany, uses the Euro (€) as its official currency. Most transactions throughout the region are conducted in euros, from larger purchases to small-scale street vendors. For international travelers, it's essential to have a basic understanding of the exchange rate before arrival, as it fluctuates over time. You can expect to get approximately 1.08 USD for 1 Euro, but this can vary.

If you're coming from countries outside the Eurozone, it's advisable to exchange some currency before your arrival, either at a bank or an exchange bureau. While it's not always necessary to exchange large amounts beforehand, it's useful to have some euros on hand for small purchases, especially in rural areas or at local markets where credit cards may not be accepted.

### ATMs and Cash Withdrawal

ATMs (or Geldautomaten in German) are widely available throughout Baden-Württemberg, particularly in major cities like Stuttgart, Freiburg, and Heidelberg, as well as in smaller towns and villages. Most ATMs are operated by large banks, including Deutsche Bank, Commerzbank, and

Unicredit, and they are easy to spot. You'll typically find them outside banks, at major train stations, and in shopping centers.

When withdrawing cash, note that many ATMs charge a fee for foreign cards, especially if you're using a card not issued by a European bank. These fees can range from €3 to €5 per transaction, depending on the ATM provider and the bank. It's recommended to withdraw larger amounts at once to minimize these fees, as smaller withdrawals will incur more charges in the long run.

For better exchange rates, try using an ATM that belongs to a large network, as it may offer a lower fee than standalone machines. Also, keep in mind that ATMs typically offer a prompt in English, so language barriers will not be a significant issue when withdrawing cash.

**Credit and Debit Cards**

Credit and debit cards are widely accepted across Baden-Württemberg, but it's important to know that the type of card and the method of payment can vary. Visa and MasterCard are the most widely accepted card brands in the region, with widespread use in both shops and restaurants. You can also use American Express, but it's less universally accepted compared to Visa and MasterCard, especially in smaller businesses.

Contactless payment has also become increasingly popular in Baden-Württemberg, with many places offering the option to tap and go for transactions under €25, though some locations may require a pin for larger amounts. Most major establishments—such as hotels, restaurants, and stores—will accept card payments, but you may encounter smaller, independent businesses (like local bakeries or kiosks) where cash is preferred, particularly in rural areas.

While you can generally rely on your cards for purchases, be aware that a few locations, such as some family-run restaurants or boutique shops, may only accept cash. If you're planning to visit such places, it's a good idea to carry enough cash with you for those situations.

## Mobile Payments

In addition to traditional credit and debit card payments, mobile payment methods such as Apple Pay, Google Pay, and PayPal are becoming increasingly common in Baden-Württemberg. Many restaurants, cafes, and shops accept these forms of payment, which are convenient for travelers who prefer to use their smartphones rather than carrying physical cards or cash.

To use mobile payments, ensure that you have an NFC-enabled smartphone, and your card or payment service is linked to the app. As with card payments, some small or rural businesses might not yet accept mobile payments, so it's always good to have a backup plan, such as a card or cash.

## Currency Exchange Services

If you find yourself in need of exchanging your currency, there are plenty of currency exchange services available in Baden-Württemberg, especially in major cities. Most exchange bureaus will charge a service fee, and the exchange rate offered can vary. Popular exchange providers include ReiseBank, located at many major train stations, and stores like Western Union. You can also exchange currency at larger banks, though they may require you to present identification, and the exchange rate might not be as favorable as those offered by specialized exchange services.

Airport currency exchange desks tend to offer less competitive rates and higher fees, so it's best to avoid changing money at the airport unless absolutely necessary. In general, you'll find better rates at local exchange offices or when using ATMs for cash withdrawals.

## Tipping Practices

While tipping is not compulsory in Germany, it is appreciated for good service. In restaurants, rounding up the bill is common, with most people leaving between 5% and 10% of the total amount. For example, if your bill is €38, you might round it up to €40. In cafes or bars, a small tip (around €1-2) is customary for service, particularly if you received good attention or had a meal.

For hotel staff, such as bellhops or housekeeping, tipping is also appreciated but not expected. A few euros for exceptional service will be enough. Taxi drivers typically expect a 5-10% tip, depending on the fare.

**Paying with Bank Transfer**

If you're planning to stay for an extended period in Baden-Württemberg or have larger payments to make (such as for accommodation), it's possible to transfer funds directly to a bank account. Many hotels, large shops, and other businesses accept payments via bank transfer, though this is typically more common for larger transactions, such as hotel deposits or booking fees for experiences and tours.

To make a bank transfer, you'll need the IBAN (International Bank Account Number) of the receiving bank and a SWIFT/BIC code for international transfers. For these types of payments, it's best to inquire directly with the business in question about the required details.

## Safety Tips & Emergency Contacts

**Health and Medical Emergencies**

- **Hospitals and Emergency Rooms**; Hospitals in Baden-Württemberg offer excellent healthcare services. The main hospitals in major cities include:
    - **University Hospital Heidelberg**; **Address:** Im Neuenheimer Feld 672, 69120 Heidelberg; **Phone:** +49 6221 56-0; This hospital provides specialized care and emergency services 24/7.
    - **Freiburg University Hospital**; **Address:** Hugstetter Str. 55, 79106 Freiburg; **Phone:** +49 761 270-0; This facility

offers comprehensive medical services including emergency treatment.
- **Pharmacies (Apotheken)**; In case you need medication or basic health supplies, pharmacies are widely available. They are typically open from 8:00 AM to 6:30 PM on weekdays, and some stay open on weekends in popular tourist areas. The universal emergency pharmacy number for after-hours service is **0800 00 22833**.
- **Emergency Numbers:**
    - **Ambulance/Medical Emergency:** 112
    - **Fire Department:** 112
    - **Police:** 110
    - **Poisoning Emergency Helpline:** 0551 19240

**Safety Tips and Precautions**

- **Crime and Scams**; While Baden-Württemberg is generally a safe region, you should still be cautious of common scams, especially in crowded areas or tourist hotspots. Avoid leaving your belongings unattended and be aware of pickpockets, particularly in train stations, airports, and busy streets. Ensure that your valuables are stored securely and use hotel safes where available.
- **Traffic Safety**; The road infrastructure in Baden-Württemberg is well-maintained, but always follow local traffic laws. In Germany, the speed limit on highways (Autobahn) can be unrestricted in parts, but caution should be exercised in populated or construction zones, where speed limits are enforced.
    - Always use seat belts, and avoid using mobile phones while driving unless you have a hands-free system.

- o   Be aware of cycling lanes, as cyclists have priority in some areas.
- **Weather and Natural Hazards**; The weather in Baden-Württemberg can vary, especially in mountainous or forested areas. In winter months, snow and ice can make roads slippery, so it is crucial to drive carefully. If hiking in the Black Forest, be mindful of weather conditions, and carry appropriate clothing and equipment for sudden weather changes.
- **Wildlife and Nature Safety**; In forested areas, such as the Black Forest, be cautious of wildlife. Although animal encounters are rare, wild boars, deer, and foxes can occasionally be found. It is advisable to avoid feeding animals and maintain a safe distance.

## Local Etiquette and Customs

**Greeting and Interaction:**

- **Handshakes** are the most common form of greeting, and they should be firm but not overpowering. While greetings like "Hallo" or "Guten Morgen" are standard, formal greetings like "Guten Tag" (Good Day) are appreciated, especially in business contexts.
- Germans value **punctuality**—being on time is considered a sign of respect. Arriving **5–10 minutes early** for appointments, meetings, or even social gatherings is advised. If you're running late, inform the person you're meeting.
- **Personal space** is valued, and Germans tend to stand at least an arm's length apart when conversing. In public spaces, avoid close contact unless you're well-acquainted with the person.

**Table Manners and Dining Etiquette:**

- **Knife and fork**: It is customary to hold the fork in the left hand and the knife in the right when eating. Never rest your hands on the edge of the table or keep elbows on it.
- **No elbows on the table**: This is considered a sign of poor manners.
- **Waiting to start eating**: It is polite to wait until everyone at the table has their food before starting to eat.
- **Cheers ("Prost")**: When making a toast, look the other person in the eye and say "Prost!" while clinking glasses. It is also customary to clink glasses before drinking, especially in social settings.

**Gift Giving:**

- When invited to someone's home, it is polite to bring a small gift such as flowers, chocolates, or wine. Gifts should be modest, as extravagant presents can make the recipient uncomfortable.
- **Gifts for children** should be simple, like books or small toys. Avoid giving white flowers, as they are typically associated with funerals in German culture.

**Tipping and Service Charges:**

- As mentioned, tipping is appreciated but not mandatory. In restaurants, rounding up the bill or leaving a 5-10% tip is common for good service. For exceptional service, tips may go as high as 15%.
- It's customary to leave a **small tip** for hotel staff or housekeeping. In taxis, rounding up the fare is sufficient.
- **Cash is King**: While credit cards are widely accepted in larger cities, many smaller establishments prefer cash. Always check

if the restaurant, hotel, or shop accepts card payments before committing.

**Public Behavior and Social Norms:**

- Germans are generally reserved in public. Loud behavior or public displays of affection may be frowned upon, especially in more rural or conservative areas.
- **Quiet in public spaces**: Conversations on public transport or in public areas should be kept at a reasonable volume. In trains, buses, and trams, phone calls should be brief and quiet.
- **Queueing**: Respecting queues is paramount, and jumping the line in public spaces like ticket counters or buses is seen as rude.

**Dress Code:**

- In general, Germans are well-dressed and take pride in their appearance. When dining at higher-end restaurants or attending cultural events, it is a good idea to dress smartly. For casual dining or sightseeing, **comfortable, weather-appropriate clothing** is recommended.
- **Conservative dress** is favored in many parts of Baden-Württemberg, particularly in smaller towns and during religious ceremonies. Visitors should cover their shoulders and knees when entering churches.

**Language:**

- While many people in Baden-Württemberg speak English, particularly in tourist areas, it is still appreciated if visitors attempt basic German phrases. Learning greetings and thank-you phrases like "Danke" (Thank you) or "Bitte" (Please) is a sign of respect.

- **Formal vs. informal**: Use the formal "Sie" when addressing strangers or older individuals, and reserve the informal "du" for friends or people your own age once invited to use it.

## Public Holidays and Festivals

1. **New Year's Day (Neujahrstag) - January 1**
   - A nationwide holiday in Germany, New Year's Day marks the start of the year. It's a day for celebration and relaxation, with public events, fireworks, and parties throughout the region. Some businesses and restaurants may open later in the day.
   - **Special Notes:** Expect quiet public transport and closed offices or smaller shops. Some restaurants may offer special New Year's menus.

2. **Good Friday (Karfreitag) - April 15 (2025)**
   - A solemn Christian holiday observed nationwide, Good Friday is a day of reflection and silence, commemorating the crucifixion of Jesus Christ. Many businesses, including some restaurants, close early, and no loud music or festivities are held in public spaces.
   - **Special Notes:** Cultural and religious events, including church services and concerts, are commonly held. Expect limited public transport schedules.

3. **Easter Monday (Ostermontag) - April 17 (2025)**
   - Following Easter Sunday, Easter Monday is a continuation of the Easter celebration. Many families take this day off to spend time together, and there are various Easter egg hunts and public events.

- **Special Notes:** Public services and public transport usually run on a regular schedule. Many shops may open, but restaurants and cafes will likely have extended hours.

4. **Labour Day (Tag der Arbeit) - May 1**
    - A nationwide celebration of workers, Labour Day is a national holiday in Germany. Expect some public demonstrations, and many businesses, especially retail shops, remain closed.
    - **Special Notes:** Expect outdoor activities such as picnics or parades. Museums and larger attractions may remain open.

5. **Ascension Day (Christi Himmelfahrt) - May 25 (2025)**
    - Ascension Day marks the ascension of Jesus Christ to heaven, and it is observed with church services and local parades. It is also celebrated as Father's Day (Vatertag), where groups of men often take part in hikes, parties, and barbecues.
    - **Special Notes:** Expect a lively atmosphere in public spaces, especially in the towns and villages where outdoor events are held. Transport schedules may vary, with certain services running on a holiday timetable.

6. **Whit Monday (Pfingstmontag) - May 29 (2025)**
    - This day commemorates the descent of the Holy Spirit and is a day of religious significance. Many towns hold festivals, fairs, and outdoor activities, with family-friendly events taking place throughout the region.
    - **Special Notes:** Expect most public services to operate normally, with many shops and restaurants open, especially in tourist areas.

7. **German Unity Day (Tag der Deutschen Einheit) - October 3**

- o This national holiday celebrates the reunification of Germany. In Baden-Württemberg, this day is marked by cultural events, political speeches, and celebrations.
- o **Special Notes:** Large public events take place, and most businesses will be closed. Museums and attractions in larger cities, such as Stuttgart, may have special events for visitors.

8. **Christmas Day (Weihnachtstag) - December 25**
   - o Christmas Day is a major holiday in Germany, celebrated with family gatherings, church services, and festive meals. It's one of the few days of the year when most businesses shut down entirely.
   - o **Special Notes:** Most restaurants that open on Christmas will offer a set Christmas menu. Public transportation will be very limited.

9. **Boxing Day (Zweiter Weihnachtstag) - December 26**
   - o Boxing Day is a day to continue the Christmas celebrations, and while most businesses are closed, some restaurants, especially in tourist areas, will remain open.
   - o **Special Notes:** Expect a quieter atmosphere compared to Christmas Eve and Day, but still with a festive mood in larger cities and towns.

**Festivals in Baden-Württemberg**

The festivals of Baden-Württemberg are an integral part of its cultural fabric. They showcase the region's history, traditions, and vibrant lifestyle. From music and food festivals to medieval celebrations, there is something for everyone throughout the year.

1. **Cannstatter Volksfest (Stuttgart Beer Festival) - Late September to Early October**
   - o Often compared to Munich's Oktoberfest, this is one of the largest beer festivals in Germany, attracting millions

of visitors. It features traditional Bavarian music, beer tents, fairground rides, and food stalls.
- **Special Notes:** The festival is family-friendly in the daytime, with dedicated areas for children and families. Be sure to try regional beers and traditional Swabian delicacies.

2. **Heidelberger Herbst - September**
    - Held in Heidelberg, this is one of the largest autumn festivals in the region. The city's medieval old town transforms into a hub of street performers, music, food stalls, and a vibrant marketplace.
    - **Special Notes:** The festival focuses on showcasing local crafts, arts, and gastronomy. It's perfect for visitors who want to experience the essence of Heidelberg's culture.

3. **Baden-Württemberg International Wine Festival - July**
    - Wine lovers will appreciate the Baden-Württemberg International Wine Festival, where regional winemakers showcase their best varieties. The festival takes place in the picturesque town of Weingarten, known for its vineyards.
    - **Special Notes:** Enjoy wine tastings, vineyard tours, and live music. Visitors can also take part in workshops on wine pairing and cultivation techniques.

4. **Freiburg Christmas Market - Late November to December 23**
    - One of the most beautiful Christmas markets in Germany, Freiburg's market features local handicrafts, delicious food, and mulled wine. The historical old town of Freiburg serves as the perfect backdrop for the festive displays.
    - **Special Notes:** Be sure to try a mug of traditional Glühwein (mulled wine) and browse for unique gifts and ornaments.

5. **Stuttgart International Festival of Animated Film - April**
    - A celebration of animation, this unique festival in Stuttgart showcases global animated films. It draws filmmakers and animators from all over the world to present their works.
    - **Special Notes:** Screenings, workshops, and discussions make this event a must for film enthusiasts. Expect events to take place at various cultural venues around the city.
6. **Ulmer Zelt Festival - June to July**
    - This summer festival is held in Ulm, located by the beautiful Danube River. It features a variety of musical performances, theatre, and circus acts, all set in a tented village.
    - **Special Notes:** Expect a wide range of live performances, from jazz to classical music, and a great selection of food and drink.
7. **Württemberg State Fair (Württembergische Landesschau) - May**
    - A celebration of Swabian culture and agriculture, this fair is held in Stuttgart and includes exhibitions of farming equipment, local food, and regional arts and crafts.
    - **Special Notes:** The fair is a great way to experience local traditions and see how the region has evolved agriculturally over the centuries.

# CHAPTER 11.

# SUGGESTED ITINERARIES

## 3-Day Itinerary: City Highlights of Stuttgart & Heidelberg

**Day 1: Exploring Stuttgart – The Heart of Baden-Württemberg**

- **Start: Stuttgart's Main Train Station (Hauptbahnhof)**; Address: Willy-Brandt-Straße 3, 70173 Stuttgart; Opening hours: 24/7; **Getting There:** Easily accessible via train from major German cities and international connections.; **Accommodation:** Hotels near the station include Park Inn by Radisson (4-star) or the budget-friendly Movenpick Hotel.

**Morning:**

- **Mercedes-Benz Museum**; Address: Mercedesstraße 100, 70372 Stuttgart; Opening hours: 9:00 AM – 6:00 PM; Entry: €10 (Adults), Free for children under 6; **Overview:** Start your day with a dive into automotive history at the world-renowned Mercedes-Benz Museum. This 16,500 square meter museum showcases over 160 vehicles and offers a fascinating journey through the evolution of the automobile.; **Must-See Highlights:** The "From the beginning" exhibit detailing the creation of the first automobile by Carl Benz, and the futuristic concept car displays.

**Lunch:**

- **Zum Paulaner**; Address: Theodor-Heuss-Straße 25, 70174 Stuttgart; Opening hours: 11:30 AM – 2:30 PM (Lunch), 5:00 PM – 11:00 PM (Dinner); Must-Taste: Swabian specialties like Zwiebelrostbraten (onion roast) and Käsespätzle (cheese noodles).; **Overview:** Enjoy hearty traditional German meals in a classic beer garden setting with local brews.

**Afternoon:**

- **Wilhelma Zoological and Botanical Garden**; Address: Wilhelma 13, 70376 Stuttgart; Opening hours: 8:15 AM – 6:00 PM (April to October), shorter hours in winter; Entry: €16 (Adults), Free for children under 6; **Overview:** After lunch, head to one of Europe's most unique zoos and botanical gardens. Wilhelma features over 1,000 species of animals and 6,000 plant species. Don't miss the historical Moorish architecture within the grounds.

**Evening:**

- **Königstraße and Schlossplatz**; **Overview:** Stroll down Stuttgart's main shopping street and visit the beautiful Schlossplatz, a large square with lush gardens and a view of the New Palace. Enjoy dinner at one of the many restaurants here, offering everything from upscale dining to casual fare.

**Day 2: Day Trip to Heidelberg – A Romantic Journey through History**; **Morning:**

- **Heidelberg Castle**; Address: Schlosshof 1, 69117 Heidelberg; Opening hours: 8:00 AM – 6:00 PM; Entry: €9 (Castle admission), €14 (with guided tour); **Overview:** Take an early train to Heidelberg (around 1 hour 20 minutes from

Stuttgart). Start your visit with Heidelberg Castle, perched high above the city with panoramic views of the Neckar River and surrounding countryside. The castle's stunning Renaissance and Baroque architecture are awe-inspiring, and the view from the castle grounds is unforgettable.; **Must-See Highlights:** The Great Barrel (the world's largest wine barrel), the castle's Pharmacy Museum, and the Knight's Hall.

**Lunch:**

- **Schlosswirtschaft**; Address: Schlosshof 2, 69117 Heidelberg; Opening hours: 11:00 AM – 10:00 PM; Must-Taste: Traditional Swabian dishes like Maultaschen (Swabian dumplings) and local wines from the region.; **Overview:** Situated just below Heidelberg Castle, this charming restaurant offers traditional regional dishes in a relaxed atmosphere.

**Afternoon:**

- **Old Bridge & Philosophenweg (Philosopher's Walk)**; **Overview:** After lunch, stroll down to the iconic Old Bridge (Alte Brücke) and cross the Neckar River. From here, head up to the Philosophenweg, a scenic walk with stunning views of the city, the river, and the castle. The path takes you through lush greenery and is dotted with interesting viewpoints, perfect for photos.
- **Heidelberg University and Old Town**; **Overview:** Explore Heidelberg's historic Old Town with its charming cobblestone streets and traditional buildings. Visit the University of Heidelberg, Germany's oldest university, and the Old University Building.

**Evening:**

- **Dinner at Vetter's Alt Heidelberger Brauhaus**; Address: Steingasse 9, 69117 Heidelberg; Opening hours: 11:00 AM – 11:00 PM; **Overview:** This renowned brewpub serves hearty German fare with house-brewed beer. Try the local beer specialty, "Vetter's Urtrunk," paired with a classic German dish like Schweinshaxe (roast pork knuckle).

**Day 3: More Stuttgart & Surrounding Scenic Views**; **Morning:**

- **Porsche Museum**; Address: Porscheplatz 1, 70435 Stuttgart; Opening hours: 9:00 AM – 6:00 PM; Entry: €10 (Adults), Free for children under 6; **Overview:** Spend your morning at the Porsche Museum to admire the sleek, high-performance cars of one of the world's most prestigious car manufacturers. Learn about the history of Porsche from its humble beginnings to becoming a global icon.

**Lunch:**

- **Restaurant Linde**; Address: Königstraße 45, 70173 Stuttgart; Opening hours: 12:00 PM – 2:00 PM (Lunch), 5:30 PM – 11:00 PM (Dinner); **Overview:** Enjoy lunch at this well-known spot offering delicious local and regional dishes in a cozy atmosphere. Don't miss the Spätzle and delicious seasonal specials.

**Afternoon:**

- **Killesberg Park**; Address: Killesbergstraße 37, 70192 Stuttgart; Opening hours: Open daily from dawn to dusk; **Overview:** Spend a relaxing afternoon exploring Killesberg Park, a large green space in Stuttgart with beautifully landscaped gardens, a small tower, and a train that takes you around the park. It's an excellent way to unwind before the final evening of your trip.

**Evening:**

- **Dinner at Das Gerber**; Address: Königstraße 28, 70173 Stuttgart; Opening hours: 10:00 AM – 9:00 PM; **Overview:** End your trip with a final dinner in one of Stuttgart's top shopping and dining centers. Das Gerber offers both fine dining and casual eats, with a focus on seasonal and local produce.

## 5-Day Itinerary: Black Forest & Lake Constance Adventure

**Day 1: Arrival in Stuttgart & Exploring the City**

- **Accommodation:**
    - **Steigenberger Graf Zeppelin**; Address: Arnulf-Klett-Platz 7, 70173 Stuttgart; Check-in: 3:00 PM | Check-out: 12:00 PM; Pricing: From €190 per night; A luxurious hotel located near Stuttgart's main train station, offering modern amenities, a spa, and a prime location for exploring the city.
- **Breakfast:**
    - **Café Krokante**; Address: Königstrasse 18, 70173 Stuttgart; Open: 8:00 AM - 5:00 PM; A charming café offering fresh pastries, coffee, and breakfast sandwiches. Known for their rich German coffee blends.
- **Morning Activity:**
    - **Mercedes-Benz Museum**; Address: Mercedesstraße 100, 70372 Stuttgart; Opening Hours: 9:00 AM - 6:00 PM (Closed Mondays); Entrance: €10; Explore the world of automotive history, featuring over 160

vehicles, from the earliest inventions to cutting-edge designs.

- **Lunch:**
    - **Café Watzke**; Address: Eberhardstr. 45, 70173 Stuttgart; Open: 10:00 AM - 8:00 PM; A cozy spot serving hearty Swabian cuisine like Spätzle and Maultaschen.
- **Afternoon Activity:**
    - **Stuttgart's Schlossplatz & New Palace**; Address: Schlossplatz 1, 70173 Stuttgart; Open: All day, free access; Visit the grand public square, explore the New Palace, and stroll through the gardens. A central spot to experience the vibrancy of the city.
- **Evening Activity:**
    - **Stuttgart State Opera**; Address: Oberer Schlossgarten 6, 70173 Stuttgart; Show Times: 7:00 PM (Varies by performance); Ticket Price: From €25; Experience an evening of world-class opera or ballet performance at one of Europe's finest opera houses.

**Day 2: Heidelberg & Wine Tasting in Baden**

- **Accommodation:**
    - **Hotel Europäischer Hof Heidelberg**; Address: Bergheimer Str. 47, 69115 Heidelberg; Check-in: 2:00 PM | Check-out: 11:00 AM; Pricing: From €150 per night; A historic luxury hotel offering elegant rooms and views of the Heidelberg Castle.
- **Breakfast:**
    - **Café Extrablatt Heidelberg**; Address: Zähringerstr. 20, 69115 Heidelberg; Open: 8:00 AM - 10:00 PM; Enjoy a

wide selection of breakfast dishes in a cozy atmosphere.

- **Morning Activity:**
  - **Heidelberg Castle**; Address: Schlosshof 1, 69117 Heidelberg; Opening Hours: 8:00 AM - 6:00 PM; Entrance: €9; Take the funicular up to the castle for panoramic views of Heidelberg, explore the impressive courtyards, and visit the German Pharmacy Museum inside the castle.
- **Lunch:**
  - **Zur Traube**; Address: Alte Brücke 3, 69117 Heidelberg; Open: 11:30 AM - 2:00 PM; Taste local Baden wines paired with traditional German dishes, such as pork knuckle and sausages.
- **Afternoon Activity:**
  - **Wine Tasting in the Baden Region**; Address: Various wineries, e.g., **Weingut Dr. Wehrheim**; Booking required in advance; Experience the best of Baden's wines, including Pinot Noir and Riesling, while enjoying the beautiful vineyard landscapes.
- **Evening Activity:**
  - **Heidelberg Old Town & Philosopher's Walk**; Stroll through the medieval streets of Heidelberg, and take a scenic walk along the Philosopher's Walk for incredible views of the town and the Neckar River.

**Day 3: Black Forest (Schwarzwald) Exploration**

- **Accommodation:**
  - **Schlosshotel Bühlerhöhe**; Address: Bühlot 1, 77815 Bühl; Check-in: 3:00 PM | Check-out: 12:00

PM; Pricing: From €220 per night; A luxurious castle hotel nestled in the Black Forest, perfect for a relaxing night amidst nature.

- **Breakfast:**
  - **Hotel Restaurant**; Offering a buffet breakfast, focusing on fresh, regional ingredients like Black Forest ham and local cheeses.
- **Morning Activity:**
  - **Triberg Waterfalls**; Address: 78098 Triberg; Opening Hours: Open all day, entrance to the museum €4; Explore Germany's tallest waterfalls and take a hike through the surrounding Black Forest trails.
- **Lunch:**
  - **Berggasthof & Hotel Brend**; Address: Brendstraße 7, 77880 Sasbachwalden; Open: 11:30 AM - 2:30 PM; Enjoy a hearty traditional Black Forest meal with views of the surrounding mountains.
- **Afternoon Activity:**
  - **Black Forest Open-Air Museum**; Address: Vogtsbauernhof 1, 77728 Gutach; Opening Hours: 9:00 AM - 6:00 PM; Entrance: €12; Explore historical farmhouses, experience traditional Black Forest life, and learn about regional crafts and agriculture.
- **Evening Activity:**
  - **Dinner at Restaurant Schwarzwaldstube**; Address: Hotel Traube Tonbach, 72270 Baiersbronn; Open: 6:30 PM - 10:00 PM; Michelin-starred restaurant offering a contemporary take on Black Forest cuisine.

**Day 4: Lake Constance & Meersburg**

- **Accommodation:**
    - **Hotel Seehof Meersburg**; Address: Ob. Schlossstr. 4, 88709 Meersburg; Check-in: 3:00 PM | Check-out: 12:00 PM; Pricing: From €140 per night; A lakeside hotel offering stunning views over Lake Constance and easy access to nearby attractions.
- **Breakfast:**
    - **Café am See**; Address: Seepromenade 8, 88709 Meersburg; Open: 8:00 AM - 6:00 PM; Enjoy breakfast with views of the lake, offering a variety of light dishes and pastries.
- **Morning Activity:**
    - **Meersburg Castle**; Address: Burgstraße 1, 88709 Meersburg; Opening Hours: 9:00 AM - 6:00 PM; Entrance: €8; Explore this medieval fortress with breathtaking views of the lake and exhibits on the region's history.
- **Lunch:**
    - **Restaurant Schiff**; Address: Seepromenade 15, 88709 Meersburg; Open: 11:30 AM - 2:30 PM; Enjoy regional specialties like fresh fish from the lake, served in a charming lakeside setting.
- **Afternoon Activity:**
    - **Ferry to Mainau Island**; Address: Mainau, 78465 Konstanz; Opening Hours: 9:00 AM - 7:00 PM (varies seasonally); Entrance: €20; Visit this lush flower island known for its botanical gardens, tropical butterflies, and peaceful walking paths.

**Day 5: Exploring the Town of Konstanz & Departure**

- **Breakfast:**
  - **Café del Sol**; Address: Bodanstr. 3, 78462 Konstanz; Open: 7:30 AM - 4:00 PM; A lively spot serving coffee, fresh pastries, and light breakfast dishes.

- **Morning Activity:**
  - **Konstanz Old Town & Imperia Statue**; Explore the historic town, visit the Konstanz Cathedral, and marvel at the Imperia statue on the harbor.

- **Lunch:**
  - **Restaurant Pier 9**; Address: Hafenstraße 3, 78462 Konstanz; Open: 11:30 AM - 2:30 PM; Enjoy a gourmet meal with a view of Lake Constance, offering fresh seafood and regional wines.

- **Departure:**; Head to the train station for your onward journey.

## 7-Day Itinerary: Best of Baden-Württemberg (Castles, Nature & Culture)

**Day 1: Arrival in Stuttgart**

- **Accommodation:**; *Park Inn by Radisson Stuttgart*; Address: Hauptstr. 26, 70563 Stuttgart; Check-in: 3:00 PM; Price: Starting from €95 per night for a standard room
- **Dining:**; *Restaurant Wielandshöhe* (Fine dining); Address: Wielandstr. 3, 70597 Stuttgart; Opening hours: 6:30 PM -

10:30 PM; Price: €45-60 per person; Must-Try: Swabian specialties like Zwiebelrostbraten

- **Attraction:**; **Mercedes-Benz Museum**; Address: Mercedesstr. 100, 70372 Stuttgart; Opening hours: 9:00 AM - 6:00 PM; Price: €10 entry; Highlight: Explore the history of automotive innovation, featuring over 160 vehicles from the Mercedes-Benz collection.
    - After visiting, stroll around Stuttgart's Schlossplatz, the city's central square surrounded by beautiful architecture.
    - Evening: Dinner at *Weinstube Kloine* in the city center for local wine and hearty food.

**Day 2: Stuttgart and Surroundings**

- **Accommodation:**; *Althoff Hotel am Schlossgarten*; Address: Schillerstr. 23, 70173 Stuttgart; Price: Starting from €140 per night
- **Attraction:**; **Stuttgart State Gallery**; Address: Konrad-Adenauer-Str. 30, 70173 Stuttgart; Opening hours: 10:00 AM - 6:00 PM; Price: €10; Highlight: Masterpieces from artists like Picasso, Van Gogh, and Rembrandt.
    - Lunch at *SchwabenQuellen* in the city center for a variety of regional specialties.
    - Afternoon: Visit **Wilhelma Zoo and Botanical Gardens**, a must-see for nature lovers.; Address: Wilhelma 13, 70376 Stuttgart; Opening hours: 8:15 AM - 6:00 PM; Price: €20; Highlight: Over 1,000 species and a beautiful park to explore.
    - Evening: Experience Stuttgart's nightlife at *The Roxy* for live music or cocktails.

### Day 3: Heidelberg - A Journey Through History

- **Accommodation:**; *Hotel Europäischer Hof Heidelberg*; Address: Friedrich-Ebert-Anlage 1, 69117 Heidelberg; Price: Starting from €130 per night

- **Attraction:**; **Heidelberg Castle**; Address: Schlossberg 1, 69117 Heidelberg; Opening hours: 8:00 AM - 6:00 PM; Price: €9; Highlight: The iconic castle offers panoramic views over the city and the Neckar River.
  - After touring the castle, enjoy lunch at *Schlosswirtschaft* on-site, known for its local fare and views.
  - Afternoon: Walk along the Old Bridge and visit the **Old Town (Altstadt)**, known for its charming shops and cafés.
  - Dinner at *Gasthaus Backmulde*, offering traditional Heidelberg cuisine.

### Day 4: Exploring the Black Forest

- **Accommodation:**; *Hotel Bareiss*; Address: Hermann-Hesse-Str. 5, 72270 Baiersbronn; Price: €240 per night
- **Attraction:**; **Triberg Waterfalls**; Address: 78098 Triberg im Schwarzwald; Opening hours: Open year-round; Price: €3; Highlight: One of Germany's tallest waterfalls, ideal for nature lovers and photographers.
  - Lunch in Triberg at *Café Schaefer*, famous for its homemade cakes.
  - Afternoon: Hike through the Black Forest's scenic trails, perhaps exploring **Schluchsee** or **Feldberg** for stunning views and nature walks.

- Dinner at *Schwabenstube* in the heart of the Black Forest, where hearty meals like roast pork and Spätzle are served.

**Day 5: Lake Constance (Bodensee)**

- **Accommodation:**; *Hotel Bad Horn*; Address: Seestr. 12, 9304 Horn, Switzerland; Price: €200 per night
- **Attraction:**; **Mainau Island (Flower Island)**; Address: Mainau, 78465 Insel Mainau; Opening hours: 9:00 AM - 7:00 PM; Price: €20; Highlight: Visit the island for beautiful botanical gardens, palaces, and scenic views of Lake Constance.
  - Lunch at *SchwabenQuellen* in Meersburg, where you can sample fresh fish from the lake.
  - Afternoon: Visit the **Meersburg Castle**, one of the oldest castles in Germany.
  - Evening: Enjoy dinner at *Seeblick* in Konstanz with lakeside views and fresh seafood.

**Day 6: Freiburg and the Black Forest Scenic Route**

- **Accommodation:**; *Schlosshotel Bühlerhöhe*; Address: Bühlerhöhe 1, 76534 Baden-Baden; Price: €190 per night
- **Attraction:**; **Freiburg Minster (Cathedral)**; Address: Münsterplatz, 79098 Freiburg; Opening hours: 9:00 AM - 6:00 PM; Price: Free; Highlight: The stunning Gothic cathedral with its beautiful stained-glass windows and panoramic city views.
  - Lunch at *Gasthaus zum Roten Bären*, one of Freiburg's oldest restaurants.
  - Afternoon: Visit **Schauinsland Mountain** for spectacular hiking and scenic cable car rides.
  - Dinner at *Restaurant Schwabenhaus* for regional Black Forest delicacies like wild boar.

**Day 7: Departure via Baden-Baden**

- **Accommodation:**; *Brenners Park-Hotel & Spa*; Address: Sophienstr. 2, 76530 Baden-Baden; Price: Starting from €340 per night
- **Attraction:**; **Caracalla Spa**; Address: Kaiserallee 1, 76530 Baden-Baden; Opening hours: 8:00 AM - 10:00 PM; Price: €25; Highlight: A luxurious spa experience with thermal baths and wellness treatments.
    - Enjoy lunch at *La Casserole* in Baden-Baden, offering French-German fusion cuisine.
    - Afternoon: Take a relaxing stroll in **Lichtentaler Allee**, a beautiful park along the Oos River.
    - Evening: Depart for your onward journey.

# CONCLUSION

## Final Travel Tips & Recommendations

**Attractions and Destinations**

Many of the region's attractions are not only historically significant but also require careful planning. For instance:

- **Heidelberg Castle**; *Address*: Schloss Heidelberg, 69117 Heidelberg; *Opening Times*: Daily from 8:00 AM - 6:00 PM (varies with seasons); *Pricing*: Entry to the castle: €9 (adults), €5 (children); *Other Info*: For a more immersive experience, consider a guided tour or the funicular ride from the city to the castle. This iconic site overlooks the Neckar River and the charming city of Heidelberg. Avoid weekends in peak season (summer) to dodge crowds.

- **Schwetzingen Palace & Gardens**; *Address*: Schloss Schwetzingen, 68723 Schwetzingen; *Opening Times*: Gardens: 8:00 AM - 6:00 PM; Palace: 9:00 AM - 5:00 PM (varies seasonally); *Pricing*: Gardens: €4, Palace: €5 (combined ticket: €8); *Other Info*: The palace's beautiful gardens are a highlight, with paths leading through meticulously designed landscapes, perfect for a peaceful afternoon stroll. Check for concert events held in the gardens during summer for a culturally enriching experience.

- **Lake Constance (Bodensee)**; *Address*: Various locations around the lake (Friedrichshafen, Konstanz,

Meersburg); *Opening Times*: The lake itself is accessible year-round; boat services operate between March and October.; *Pricing*: Boat tours: from €20 per person; *Other Info*: The lake is ideal for cycling and hiking. The ferry between Germany, Switzerland, and Austria also adds an international dimension to your visit. Be sure to check ferry schedules in advance, especially during peak times.

**Dining Options**

Baden-Württemberg's cuisine is a central part of its identity. As you explore, you'll come across a mix of hearty Swabian dishes and innovative culinary experiences. Here are some local dining options to consider:

- **Best Restaurants**:
    - *Restaurant Schlossberg* (Heidelberg) – An upscale dining experience offering gourmet takes on regional classics. Expect to pay around €50-€70 per person.
    - *Gasthof Stern* (Stuttgart) – A beloved traditional Swabian restaurant, known for Maultaschen and Spätzle, priced around €20-€30 per person.
    - *Café Extrablatt* (Freiburg) – A cozy café perfect for brunch, with an extensive menu that caters to all tastes at affordable prices (€10-€15).
    - *Zum Goldenen Hirschen* (Baden-Baden) – A Michelin-starred option for a refined experience with a focus on seasonal ingredients. Expect to spend about €80 per person for a tasting menu.
- **Must-Taste Cuisines**:; The region is famed for its hearty dishes. Don't leave without trying **Maultaschen** (Swabian dumplings), **Spätzle** (egg noodles), and the iconic **Schwarzwälder Kirschtorte** (Black Forest Cake). For a unique

experience, opt for **Flammkuchen** – an Alsatian-style pizza popular in the region, especially in wine-growing areas.

**Accommodation Recommendations**

The accommodation in Baden-Württemberg caters to all preferences and budgets. Here's a breakdown of the best options:

- **Luxury Stays**:
    - *Brenners Park-Hotel & Spa* (Baden-Baden) – A five-star hotel with a luxurious spa and fine dining. Rates start around €300 per night.
    - *Althoff Hotel am Schlossgarten* (Stuttgart) – A perfect blend of elegance and modernity, located near the city center. Rates start around €200 per night.
- **Mid-Range Options**:
    - *Park Inn by Radisson* (Heidelberg) – Located by the river with easy access to Heidelberg Castle. Rates start around €120 per night.
    - *Holiday Inn Express* (Freiburg) – Offers modern, affordable accommodation with access to the old town. Rates from €90 per night.
- **Budget-Friendly**:
    - *Hostel Heidelberg* – A simple, budget-friendly option near the city center. Expect rates from €25 per night for a dormitory bed.
    - *Hotel Central* (Stuttgart) – A basic but comfortable hotel in Stuttgart, starting at €60 per night.

**Practical Tips for Travelers**

1. **Cash & Payments**: While credit cards are widely accepted, some smaller towns and local markets may only accept cash

(Euro). Ensure you have cash on hand for small purchases and public transportation. ATMs are easy to find in all cities.

2. **Language**: German is the official language, and although many people speak English, especially in tourist areas, learning basic German phrases like "Guten Morgen" (Good morning) or "Wie viel kostet das?" (How much is this?) can enrich your experience.

3. **Public Holidays**: Many businesses, especially restaurants and shops, close on Sundays or during public holidays like Easter, Christmas, and New Year's. Plan your activities accordingly and check ahead for opening hours.

4. **Weather Considerations**: Baden-Württemberg has a temperate climate. Summer can get warm, especially in cities like Stuttgart and Heidelberg, so pack light clothing. In winter, the region can experience snowfall, particularly in the Black Forest. Always check weather forecasts before hiking or engaging in outdoor activities.

# TRAVEL REFLECTIONS

Printed in Great Britain
by Amazon